BASEBALL COACH'S

GUIDE

and *Skills*

TO

Drills

BASEBALL COACH'S

GUIDE

TO

Drills and Skills

by **Danny Litwhiler**

Baseball Coach
Department of Physical Education
and Recreation
Florida State University
Tallahassee, Florida

•

Illustrated by John O. Wilkinson

PRENTICE-HALL, INC., ENGLEWOOD CLIFFS, N. J.

Baseball Coach's Guide to Drills and Skills, by Danny Litwhiler
© 1963 by Prentice-Hall, Inc., Englewood Cliffs, N. J.

Library of Congress Catalog Card Number: 63-10664

PRINTED IN THE UNITED STATES OF AMERICA
05630—BC

Dedicated to:

Dr. E. H. Nelson
Bloomsburg, Pennsylvania

My college coach, whose faith in me inspired and guided me through my baseball career. It is with his personal example in mind that I undertake the coaching of others, with the hope that these others will help perpetuate his ideals of coaching.

DRILLS, DRILLS, DRILLS!

The baseball coach was mighty tough,
He never seemed to get enough
Of drill, and drill, and drill, and drill,
Until it seemed he wished to kill.
The players made a lot of fuss,
And said, "*He's making fools of us.*
Now what's the use of all that stuff?
We know those plays all well enough.
If he would let us play a game
We'd use all those plays just the same."
At last there came the longed-for day
When they had THE big game to play.
And then those weeks of constant drill
Began to show in baseball skill.
The team would make their double plays
And shine in lots of other ways.
They'd catch a runner off at first
The way they often had rehearsed.
And if one tried a hit to stretch
They always got the sorry wretch.
And when they came to bat themselves,
They acted like some sprightly elves.
They made their double steals with ease,
And did about just as they'd please.
They bunted in a man from third,
And made the pitcher look absurd.
And when the game was played and won,
They said, "*Oh boy, but that was fun.*
Hey, Coach, we want to drill some more,
And next time make a bigger score."

Written and contributed by
RAYMOND F. BELLAMY

PREFACE

"Baseball players are born; stars are made"—made by the efforts of hard-working, imaginative coaches and the individual efforts of players. It was this thought that dominated and gave direction to the writing of *Baseball Coach's Guide to Drills and Skills*.

It is impossible to develop as a baseball player without proper drills and a thorough knowledge of the skills involved. A good coach can recognize the correct drills needed to develop a team and can adapt or develop a drill for any problem which faces him. Players must practice the strong points, of course, but repetition of drills on the weak points results in a superior team.

The drills in this book have all been tried and proven to be of value to some player, college coach, or major league manager. Not all the drills can be used by every player or team, and it is advisable to select the drills best suited to individual and team needs.

This book could not have been written without my association, as a major league player and coach, with such men as *Bob Elliott, Bucky Harris, Fred Hutchinson, Danny Murtaugh, Stan Musial, Bobby Bragan, Luke Sewell, Billy Southworth, Al Lopez,* and *Ted Williams*. Also, I cannot overlook the impact of being a college coach and observing, as well as absorbing, the knowledge and ways of the coaches in the American Association of College Baseball Coaches.

Credit must be given to the following men who have contributed to the completion of *Baseball Coach's Guide to Drills and Skills:* Don Fauls, Trainer; Keith Pitchford, Director of Intramurals for Men; and Ernie Lanford, Freshman Baseball Coach—all of the Florida State University—and ex-Dodger Trainer, Doc Harold Wendler. Discussing and working with these drills during the Baseball Coaching Theory class at Florida State also proved very beneficial.

D.W.L.

TABLE OF CONTENTS

NOTE TO THE READER: The symbols on this page are the same for each of the applicable Drills, and the key below may be used as a single reference to determine functions and positions.

KEY

(R) BASE RUNNER

(X) COACH

(F) FUNGO HITTER

(H) HITTER

(P) PLAYER OR PICK UP MAN

(1)-(9) NUMERICAL POSITIONS

〰〰〰➤ GROUND BALL

───➤ PATH OF BASE RUNNER

───┤ PATH OF DEFENSIVE PLAYER

- - - -➤ THROWN BALL OR FLY BALL

BASEBALL COACH'S

GUIDE

and *Skills*

TO

Drills

CHAPTER 1

BASEBALL
TRAINING AND
FIRST AID

Preparation for a baseball season requires that the players start preliminary work on their own about a month before regular practice sessions begin. In order for players to be ready for the opening practice, they must spend time and effort to get into condition. Pre-practice work should be divided into four categories: running, stretching, throwing, and weight work.

There are some injuries which can be anticipated in baseball practice and games. Since all coaches must know the first aid requirements for these injuries, we shall cover very briefly the prevention and first aid of baseball injuries.

It should be mandatory for every player to have a complete physical examination by a competent physician prior to the first practice of the season, at which time tetanus shots must be given.

1. Running

Early conditioning requires plenty of running. The only way for any player to develop speed and stamina is to run, run, run. *Good legs make good ball players.* Running is hard work and demands initiative and self-sacrifice. This applies to all players, but especially to pitchers. Remember, it is possible to play with a sore arm, but practically impossible to play ball with a sore leg. *Suggested drills: Nos. 11-17, 19.*

2. Stretching

All parts of the body need stretching. Stretching exercises will prevent muscle pulls in the legs and back, and all players, especially pitchers, should stretch their arms.

Suggested drills: Nos. 20-24, 27.

3. Throwing

After stretching well, start throwing easily. You can test and find out how much easier it is to throw after a good arm stretch. You should throw every day, but do not throw hard until the arm is warmed up. Pitchers in early season practices should not throw hard for a week, but should start spinning curves the first day. Don't try to break them off; just spin the ball to get the feel.

Suggested drills: Nos. 27-28, 31-34, 91-93.

4. Weight Work

Working with weights is not designed to develop bulging muscles, but to develop muscle tone. The following is a tentative program:

Get a barbell or any 10- to 15-pound weight that is easy to control. Standing, with the arm at the side in full extension, palm up, weight in hand, flex the arm slowly to complete flexion. Return to full extension. Do this 10 times. This exercise strengthens the anterior arm muscles, above the elbow. (Note Illustration No. 1, Figure No. 1.) Then, in the same basic position, but with the lower arm in the midway position (thumb pointing up), repeat the above exercise 10 times. This also strengthens arm muscles *above the elbow.* (Note Illustration No. 1, Figure No. 2; *see next page.*)

To strengthen muscles in the *back of the arm,* above the elbow: Raise the arm above the shoulder with elbow bent (flexed); straighten arm 10 times. (Note Illustration No. 1, Figure No. 3.) To strengthen muscles of the arm *below the elbow:* Rest elbow and lower arm on a table with the wrist extending over the end of the table, weight in hand, palm up; flex the wrist 10 times. These muscles are most impor-

3

2

ILLUS. NO. 1

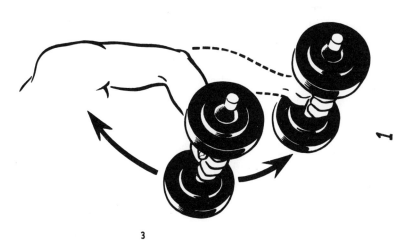

1

3

tant for wrist action in throwing the curve ball or any breaking pitch. (Note Illustration No. 2, Figure No. 1.) Hold the weight with thumb pointing up. Spin the weight to the right and back to the left 10 times. (Note Illustration No. 2, Figure No. 2.) This exercise strengthens the rotator muscles of the wrist and elbow.

Turn the hand over, with wrist flexed, so that it faces the floor; extend wrist. Do this 10 times (Note Illustration No. 2, Figure No. 3.)

The exercises above are to be done only three days per week. Add one repetition to each exercise per week. In other words, each exercise is done 10 times per day, three days a week. The next week each exercise is done 11 times per day, three days per week, and so on until 20 repetitions per day are reached. This can be continued indefinitely; however, it is recommended that all weight work be done *after* practice, never before.

5. Tips for Pitchers

Pitchers should do their running just before going into the club house at the end of practice. However, prior to a game, pitchers who are not going to work that day should run while the other team is taking batting practice or else immediately following the game. In this way the player works up a good sweat and changes his shirt or goes in; he does not stand around in a damp sweat shirt which may lead to a sore arm. All pitchers should have at least two sweat shirts. Prior to a workout on a cold, windy day, it is advisable to put oil on the arm, shoulder, and back. After a good workout or after pitching a game, pitchers should get a massage on the arm, shoulder, and back muscles with alcohol. This is done to close the pores and to prevent sore arms. This massage should be of short duration—only enough to close the pores.

Pitchers, as well as all other players, should play plenty of "pepper" games. This helps to develop quick reflexes. Also, these games are good exercise, good for stomach muscles and over-all conditioning. (Note Drill No. 29.)

Many pitchers develop a blister on the thumb side of the middle finger of the pitching hand. This is caused by the pressure exerted on the ball by this finger, especially when throwing the curve ball. The fingernail is always pointed in this area. When pressure is exerted on the ball, as in throwing the curve, the point of the nail projects into the

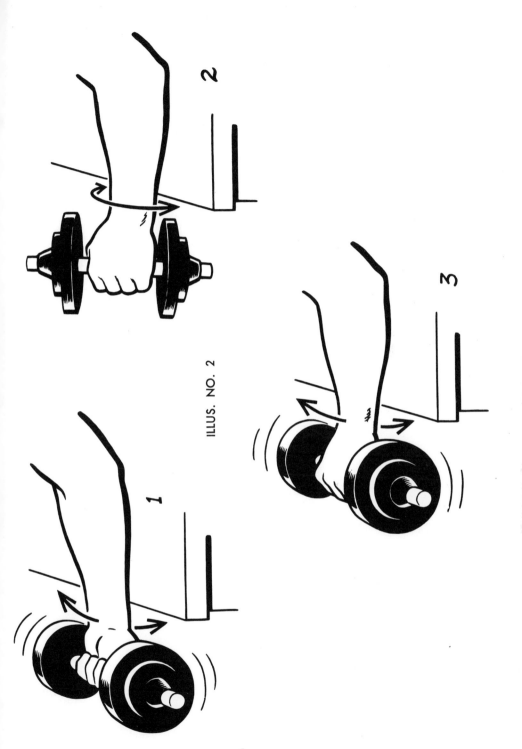

ILLUS. NO. 2

5

skin, causing a blister to form. This condition can be eliminated by keeping this point of the nail filed down. Never use clippers on this nail. Use a nail file.

6. Emergencies on the Field

Any player hit on the head with a pitched or thrown ball should be carefully examined before he is moved or his head raised. If injury is severe, the player may be unconscious, eyes dilated, or bleeding from the ear. Any or all of these symptoms may be present. If so, call a physician, apply ice, and don't let the player stand up or raise his head more than necessary for his comfort. Any severe fracture can be seen immediately, for the fractured area will be distorted. The utmost care should be exercised to prevent further injury. Splint the part and send the player to the hospital as soon as possible. A catcher's shin guard makes as fine a splint as one could use. (Note Illustration No. 3.)

In case of a spike wound:

A. If a *scratch wound*—use disinfectant and sterile bandage. Allow player to continue playing.

B. If a *puncture wound*—stop bleeding, use disinfectant and sterile bandage, if possible, to continue playing. If sutures are required use sterile bandage and take player to doctor.

7. Treatment for Strawberries

Shave the area around the wound, and paint the shaved area with "Tuf-skin" or benzoin. Cover a sterile gauze pad with a good ointment (Zinc Oxide) and place on top of the wound. Place two or three extra gauze pads on top of the first pad. Tape this to the skin, starting at the bottom and going up. You now have an extra sliding pad over the injured area. Also, the wound will heal from the inside out, eliminating a scab.

8. General Comments on Injury Prevention

◆ All players should wear helmets while batting. It is a must for catchers and pitchers to wear protective cups, and infielders should wear them. It may be optional for outfielders.

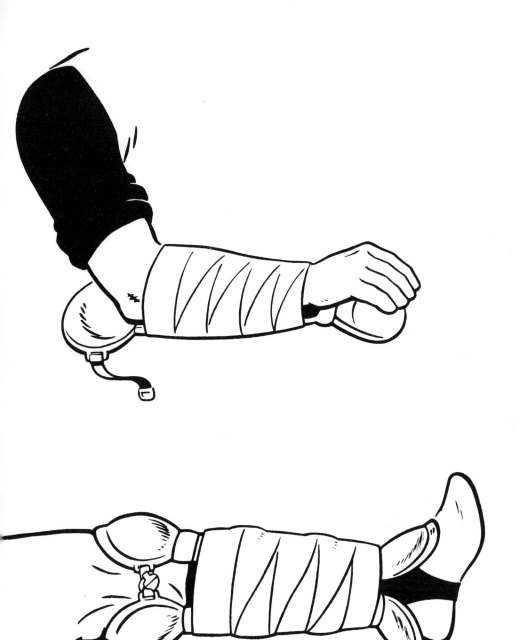

ILLUS. NO. 3

7

- Long Jockey-type shorts, cut off at the knees and worn under the supporter, are ideal to prevent jock itch and slide burns.
- Players who get frequent blisters on the fingertips should use "Tuf-skin" or benzoin on them. This will toughen the skin.
- For all bruises or sprains, apply ice or one of the new quick-cold compresses to the affected area. (*Kwick-Kold* or Ethyl Chloride)
- Never let a player participate when possible permanent injury may result.
- Caution should be used to keep players and spectators out of the danger area of a batted or thrown ball and the swinging area of a fungo hitter and a hitter swinging at a pitched ball. A bat that slips out of a batter's hand is a lethal weapon.

9. Breaking in New Shoes

There are two principal methods of breaking in new shoes so they will be comfortable and fit properly.

The first way is to rub Vaseline into the inside of the heel of the shoe until it becomes soft, pliable, and comfortable.

The second, and probably the best, method is to break down the heel with the hand. Then, insert the large end of a bat in the inside of the heel of the shoe and press down hard, bouncing it against a wooden surface, followed by rubbing hand soap on the inside of the heel. This should condition the shoe for comfortable wear.

New shoes should be broken in slowly. At first they should *not* be worn throughout an entire practice period and should not be worn while sliding. Short periods of wear are best until they become shaped to the player's feet.

10. Choosing and Breaking in a New Glove

In choosing a glove, size and style will be determined by the player's position. In his choice of glove, the player should be guided by the following: Pitchers need a large glove, and catchers need a large glove (mitt) with a flexible, open pocket. Outfielders, third basemen and shortstop should choose a medium-sized glove. Second basemen need a small glove with a big pocket, and first basemen require a large glove with an open pocket.

After the proper selection has been made, the following steps should be taken in the process of breaking in the glove:

- Soak the glove in water for several minutes.
- Remove the glove from the water; place it on your glove hand in the manner you want it to fit, and pound it into shape with the other hand. Then, when it is shaped to fit your hand, play catch with it.
- In storing the glove for the night, place a ball in the pocket, shape the glove around the ball, and wrap string or rubber bands around the glove to hold it in place.
- In about three days the glove should be ready for use in a game. Occasionally, use saddle soap on the glove. It may not be sanitary, but spit goes a long way in keeping a good pocket in a glove. Whereas a dry glove lets a ball spin out, a damp glove will hold it.

CHAPTER 2

CONDITIONING

DRILLS

The coach is primarily interested in getting his players in good physical and mental condition so they will be able to function well on the field. To accomplish this, running and leg exercises will make up most of the conditioning drills.

A ball player is only as good as his legs. He can play well with a weak or sore arm, bad hand or finger, or even with a headache or stomach trouble. But with a sore leg, foot, or ankle he loses 25 to 90 percent of his usefulness to his club. We therefore want to get his legs in shape first; then his arms will come along easier and with less chance of injury.

The coach must convince the players of the value of conditioning drills. Most players hate these drills, especially calisthenics. Therefore, interesting drills must be used to take the place of routine, organized calisthenics. Once a player takes pride in his physical condition and disciplines himself to get in shape and stay in shape, he will be a real asset to the team. Several hard workers can have a positive effect on the whole team, making it a hard-working club.

If practiced correctly, the following drills will build the player physically and mentally to enter a season in excellent shape, and will keep him in good condition all year.

11. Football Pass Drill

Purpose

Especially good for pitcher conditioning, this drill is also valuable for the rest of the team.

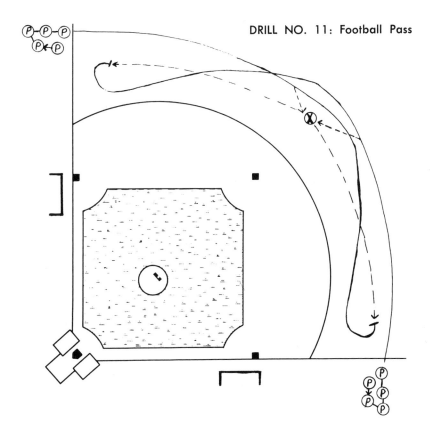

DRILL NO. 11: Football Pass

Procedure

The coach assumes a position near the edge of the infield, behind the base. Taking a starting position along the edge of the infield grass on the right field foul line, each player holds a baseball in his hand. At the signal to start, a player runs past the coach, handing him the ball as he passes by. After the player runs along the edge of the infield and progresses to the vicinity of the left field foul line, the coach yells, "cut," which is a signal for the player to cut toward home plate and receive a "football pass" from the coach.

When each player has had his turn, he lines up along the left field foul line, and retraces his path past the coach, giving him the baseball again and receiving it in the same manner along the right field line.

This drill progresses from a slow jog at short distances to long, hard-running end-zone passes beyond the foul lines. Twenty to twenty-five of these passes per day should be sufficient.

12. Rolling Semicircle

Purpose

Valuable to all as a conditioner and especially beneficial to pitchers, it can be used at any time during the practice period. Players should wear their gloves while performing the drill.

Procedure

A semicircle with a radius of approximately 12 feet is run around the coach or another player. The coach, or another player, who is facing the fielding player rolls the ball on the ground for him to field and return. Each time, the coach returns the rolling ball to a position at the opposite side of the semicircle. This is repeated 20 to 25 times for each player. After one week of practice the number should be stepped up to 50 times.

Note: Two players can easily pair off and work with each other on this drill without the aid of the coach. (Note Illustration No. 4.)

13. Fifty-Fifty Drill

Purpose

An excellent team or individual conditioner with which to end a day's practice, this is really a series of activities to be performed as follows:

ILLUS. NO. 4

12 FEET

Procedure

a. Jog 50 yards and walk back to the starting point. Repeat five times.

b. At starting point, place hands on hips, breathe deeply through the nose and exhale through the mouth.

c. Monkey squat and bounce 10 times. This is performed by doing a deep knee bend, one squat with one hand touching the ground in front of the body, followed by holding this position and bouncing.

d. Stand erect on one leg. Relax and shake other leg vigorously to feel the muscles vibrate and bounce along the bone. Repeat with the other leg.

e. Again, sprint 50 yards and walk back to the starting point. Repeat five times.

f. Repeat deep breathing as above. Monkey squat 10 times and shake legs.

g. Run fast for 50 yards and walk back to the starting point. Do this five times.

Increase the number of everything in this drill as the season advances and as players' legs are better conditioned.

14. Shift and Toss

Purpose

To improve fielding ability this drill may be executed before, during or after the regular practice period.

Procedure

A. Two players stand 10 to 15 feet apart and throw grounders at each other, bouncing them right at the other player's feet. Each backs up a few steps after a few throws until a maximum of 30 feet is reached.

This is a time to have fun and to be fancy with the glove. Spear the ball backhanded and with the glove held around back of the leg. As a means to making the season more lively, the participants may compete for Cokes, with the player making the most errors being the loser.

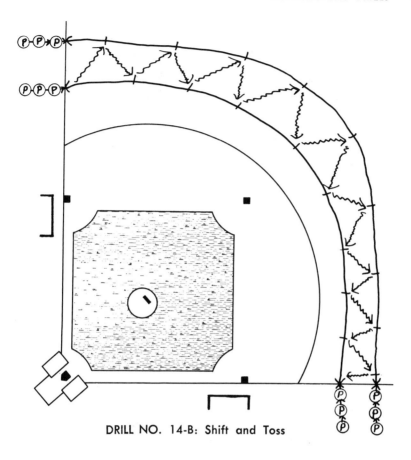

DRILL NO. 14-B: Shift and Toss

B. The outfielder version of the drill is to start two players at the left field foul line about 25 feet apart. One player rolls the ball out in front of the other player who fields the ball and returns it on the ground out in front of the player. This continues over to the right field line. This drill is done at a medium running speed and continues back and forth several times.

15. Reaction Drill

Purpose

To develop reflexes and condition the body.

Procedure

Two players, or a player and the coach, stand approximately 12 feet apart, each holding a baseball in his hand. As player A tosses the ball on the ground to one side of player B, player B tosses his ball to one side of A. Each tosses the ball so that the other must change position and tries to make him break rhythm. After 10 tosses for each player at 12 feet, the distance should be gradually increased to a maximum of 30 feet. Continue this drill at 30 feet until the player or players yell, "Uncle."

It is advisable that each player wear his glove.

If the coach is tossing the ball he can stand still while the players do the running.

16. Step on Bench Drill

Purpose

To develop and condition the legs for a long baseball season.

Procedure

Stand in front of a bench 17 to 19 inches high. Alternately place feet on the bench in rhythmic movement of the legs and arms. Do this twenty-five times for each foot. This can be done daily during pre-season training. It is advisable to discontinue it during regular season play and use running drills instead. (Note Illustration No. 5 *on next page.*)

17. Jump Rope

Purpose

The purpose of the rope jump drill is to develop the legs of baseball players for the spring needed in the performance of many plays.

Procedure

Using a standard jumping rope, make a game out of jumping. Jump to music or to your own rhythm. Use a running step and a two-leg hop. Stay up on your toes. Turn the rope forward and backward. In fact, try different ways of turning the rope. Really enjoy the drill. It is a wonder-

ILLUS. NO. 5

17

ful conditioner for pre-season work. Five to ten minutes per day, or 150 jumps per day are about right, depending upon your condition and the time available.

18. Use of Ankle Weights and Weighted Innersoles

Purpose

To increase speed, strengthen legs, help in recovering from some injuries, and to act as a psychological booster.

Procedure

The amount of weight on each foot should be no more than two or three pounds. Weights should be worn for a short workout of running and exercising before the regular practice period and for longer periods at the end of the practice session, or on one's own time. Workouts with ankle weights during the winter months are beneficial and should be encouraged.

Weighted innersoles are on the market and very practical for this work. Some coaches find them more practical than spat-type ankle weights.

19. Base Running for Time

Purpose

To increase speed of base running.

Procedure

The speed of your base runners is timed with a stop watch after players are in shape. Usually, this is the second week that they are out-of-doors. The watch should be started with the crack of the bat.

A good time for adult players to make first base is between 3.5 and 4.3 seconds. The best time recorded for a right handed player is 3.3 seconds, and the best for a left handed batter is 3.1 seconds. The following are considered good times to the other bases: from home to second base in eight seconds, to third in 12, and the complete circuit in 16 seconds. (Note Drill No. 196.)

The following directions should be used in increasing the speed of runners on the base paths:

a. Hit the bag with either foot, but never break stride.
b. Curve out to your right slightly before reaching the bag.
c. Use the bag as a pivot to avoid making big turns.
d. Lean in toward the infield as you hit the bags and move around them.

20. Stretching Drill

Purpose

To stretch the muscles of the arms and shoulders. It is particularly valuable when performed after practice hours and during the off-season. When the drill is executed after workout, it helps alleviate stiffness that might result from the practice period.

Procedure

To perform the drill, a high bar or some similar object which will support a player's weight is needed. It should be high enough for a person to hang by his hands from it without touching the floor.

Grasp the bar with one hand and hang with the arm straight, but do not try to pull up. Rotate the body clockwise, then counterclockwise. Remain in this hanging position for about 30 seconds, and then hang with the other hand grasping the bar for the same time. Follow by hanging by both hands for the same amount of time as for one hand. Increase the hanging time for each hand each time until a maximum of one minute for a hand is reached. Execute the drill twice daily, either after practice or during the day or night.

Suggested drills: Nos. 20-25, 28, 54

21. Instant Arm and Back Stretch

Purpose

In this drill the purpose is to give the ball player a quick stretch prior to play or workout. It is advisable to go no further than the exercises recommended here unless directed and supervised by a competent trainer.

Procedure

A. With both of your hands, hold another player's fingers on his right hand. As you pull his hand until his arm is extended, have him relax his entire arm, hand, and fingers, while you shake them vigorously. He must pull away from the person doing the shaking. Alternate with the other hand, allowing only a few seconds on each hand.

B. As you approach the player's back, he reaches up and interlocks the fingers of both hands behind his neck. Standing at his back, reach under his armpits passing your right hand up under his right arm and your left hand up under his left arm. Your hands then interlock on top of his hands behind his neck.

Ask the player to completely relax his entire body, take a deep breath, then blow it out. When he has exhaled, pick him up, allowing his body to curl over your chest as you lean slightly backward. Give a short bounce to his body, and the spinal column will loosen up with a popping or snapping sound. One good snap should be sufficient.

C. To strengthen the back and also to loosen it, lie on the end of a bench with hips and legs on the bench. The top part of the body extends over the end of the bench. Another man sits on or pins his legs to the bench as the player, lying first on his stomach and then on his back, moves his torso up and down.

22. Preventing a Charley Horse

Purpose

To loosen up the muscles of the upper leg, this drill should be used before any hard running or sprinting.

Procedure

Relaxed and in a standing position, the player with his left hand supports his weight against a stationary object such as a post or wall. Keeping the upper part of the right leg straight, the player flexes the leg at the knee. He grasps the instep of his right foot with the fingers of the right hand and exerts pressure upward and backward in a steady pull toward the buttocks, causing the thigh muscles to stretch and loosen up.

This same maneuver is performed with the other hand and foot. With each leg the foot should be pulled as far as possible and held for approximately five seconds. The exercise should be done alternately right and left, three to five times for each leg.

23. Groin Strengthener

Purpose

To strengthen the muscles of the groin region and thus help prevent groin injuries.

Procedure

In a sitting position, the player places his left palm against the inside of his right knee and his left elbow against the inside of his left knee. While in this position, he tries to push his knees together tightly for six seconds. Next, he leans over and grasps his outer right knee with his left hand and his outer left knee with his right hand. While holding his knees together with his hands, he tries to force them apart with leg muscles for six seconds. This drill is best when executed by alternating the exercise, first pushing the knees inward four times, then pushing them outward four times for six seconds each at maximum effort.

24. Shoulder-Loosening Drills

Purpose

For loosening tight shoulders of ball players.

Procedure

A. The first drill is performed by the player's placing his fingertips on top of his shoulders—right hand to right shoulder, left hand to left shoulder, extending his elbows and rolling his shoulders from front to back and back to front.

B. The second drill is executed with the use of a baseball bat. The player grasps the bat at each end, passes it up and over the head and down behind his shoulders and back without letting go of it. Three or four repetitions at any one time should be sufficient.

25. Abdomen Reducer

This is an exercise that you should do in your spare time and at your own convenience.

Simply suck in your stomach and hold it for a count of three. Repeat this about 25 times daily and watch your waistline reduce. It will permit you to have better hip action. It should give hips faster hip action and keep that pitcher from having a "lazy hip" when he pivots off the rubber on his follow-through delivery.

26. Rubber Ball Squeeze

Purpose

For the development of wrists and forearms.

Procedure

The drill involves the squeezing of the rubber ball, digging the fingers in, and flexing the muscles of the hand, wrist, and forearm. The number of repetitions should be increased with each drill.

Inexpensive, convenient, and not time consuming, this drill is used by many major league ball players today. Recognizing its value, some players carry a rubber ball with them and perform the drill daily.

27. Arm Strengthener and Conditioner

Purpose

To strengthen the throwing arm and to condition it for the season.

Procedure

After a warm-up period of calisthenics on the first day of practice, the squad should be arranged in pairs, with half of the squad along the first base line and the other half between third and second. In this manner, the pairs of players face each other at a distance of approximately 90 feet.

From this distance, partners throw to each other until their arms are loose, which usually takes about five minutes. Then they are ready

DRILL NO. 27: Arm Strengthener and Conditioner

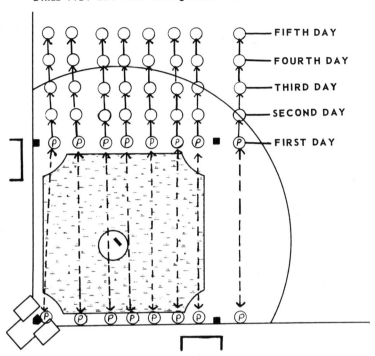

to throw three hard ones, but there should be some easy tosses between the hard throws. This ends the drill for the first day. It should take only eight to ten minutes.

On the second day, players should line up in the same manner but at a distance of 100 feet and proceed as on the previous day.

This drill should be continued for two weeks with the distance being increased by 10 feet each day to a maximum of 150 feet for pitchers and infielders, and to 250 feet for outfielders.

28. Isometric Rope Drill

Purpose

To strengthen the arm.

ILLUS. NO. 6

Procedure

The isometric rope drill should be executed after the practice session is completed, or during the off-season and only once a day.

Attach a piece of rope five feet long around a door knob or other stationary object at approximately that height, and wind the other end around your hand or wrist. Then follow the steps listed below.

 a. Assume a pitcher's position with both body and arm as you would in your first motion to pitch. Pull against the rope with maximum effort for six seconds.

 b. Attain a position of half way through the delivery and repeat the exercise.

 c. Finally, set your arm and hand at the downward follow-through position and repeat the exercise. (Note Illustration No. 6.)

29. The Pepper Game

The pepper game can be beneficial to fielders and batters. It provides practice for the batter in keeping his eye on the ball and in place hitting. The drill gives the fielder practice in fielding and should sharpen his reflexes. It never involves more than three fielders and one hitter in any one group.

Fielders should line up about 20 feet from the batter and two to three yards apart, so that they will have room to make plays to either side. The batter attempts to hit balls to the players consecutively. After the batter has hit 20 or 25 balls to each player, the player at the head of the line becomes the batter, and the original batter becomes a fielder at the foot of the line. Rotate fielders and hitters. Another way to work the drill is for the fielder at the head of the line to become the hitter when the group has fielded 25 balls without an error.

The pepper game is one of the few times when a player should attempt to get fancy with his glove. He should try out all of his novelty catches and really enjoy himself, but at the same time he should try to improve his fielding skills and strengthen his weaknesses.

For motivation and to make the pepper game more interesting, the group could play for Cokes. If the fielders catch 25 balls without error, the batter owes each fielder a Coke. However, if a fielder makes an error, he owes the batter a Coke. If the hitter hits the ball over the fielder's head, or fails to hit the ball, he owes the fielder a Coke.

30. Sports Which Enhance Baseball Ability

In the development of a baseball player, all drills do not have to be of the baseball type. In fact, many sports help to develop a baseball player to his highest capacity. If a player participated in baseball the year round, he would soon tire of it. We advise players to play other sports. Naturally, some sports are better than others for baseball development. Basketball, golf, handball, tennis, volleyball, soccer, badminton, ice skating, track, swimming, table tennis, cork ball, hiking, bowling, and numerous others are beneficial when played in the off-season. However, it would be best to avoid participation in these sports during the playing season.

Football is left off the list because it can hardly be recommended as a sport which will enhance a baseball career, although it does not harm the young player except for possible injury. If a football player continues to participate in some of the sports mentioned he should loosen up the shoulder muscles which are so vital to the skills used by baseball players. Too much football in fall and spring practice has a tendency to tighten the shoulder muscles. For this reason, we recommend playing other sports during the off-season.

There are individual drills for various positions, but the following drills are ideal for all players. Many are designed to develop the same fundamentals for each player. The coach should discuss individual drills with the player involved and should advise him how to work on his own. However, the coach should work closely with team combination drills, seeing that they do not last too long and that they are worked with zest.

CHAPTER 3

TEAM DRILLS

31. Rhythm Warm-Up—Catching and Throwing

Purpose

To develop rhythm in the catching and throwing motion.

Procedure

The drill is executed with pairs of players playing catch at approximately 50 feet. After a rhythmic pattern is developed, the players throw from a greater distance and add Drill No. 32.

In the development of a rhythmic pattern, the right handed player should concentrate on the following factors:

a. Step forward with the right foot as the ball approaches and catch it just as the right foot touches the ground.

b. Transfer the ball to the right hand as soon as it strikes the glove.

c. Step forward with the left foot, and at the same time release the ball, originating the throw from the right foot.

d. Then, the player should back up a few feet to the position where he originally started the throw, since he usually moves forward a few feet in the process of catching and throwing.

For the left handed player, the movements are reversed. That is, the left foot comes forward when catching, and the throw originates from the left foot.

All the steps mentioned should be repeated until a satisfactory rhythmic pattern has been developed. When distance is needed along with rhythm, use the crow-hop as described in Drill No. 34.

32. Pre-Warm-Up Quick Grip and Throw

Purpose

To develop in the player the habit of catching the ball, gripping it properly, and throwing as quickly as possible.

Procedure

Have players use this drill while playing catch as a warm-up for the regular practice session or preceding a game. Players should begin the drill at 40-45 feet apart and should gradually back up to a maximum of 90 feet as their arms loosen. Outfielders should lengthen this distance to about 120 feet.

The right handed player should catch the ball while stepping to meet it just as his right foot strikes the ground. He then quickly grips the ball in his right hand and throws as he strides and shifts his weight to the left foot. The feet and hands are reversed for the left handed player. The whole action is one continuous motion with the ball being snapped out of the glove and gripped as quickly as possible. The player, in order to increase control, should always throw at an object.

33. Control Development

Purpose

To increase or develop the player's control of the ball when throwing.

Procedure

All players should concentrate on the factors involved in this drill every time they throw. The principal factor is that of throwing at an object such as the catching. partner's head, shoulder, stomach, or knee. Vary the object. For example, throw two or three times at the partner's head, then follow with two or three throws at each part of his anatomy mentioned above. The player should fix his eyes on the object at which he is aiming. *Never throw unless you throw at something.*

34. Crow-Hop and Throw Drill

Purpose

To improve the throwing accuracy of both infielders and outfielders in the overhand throw, the crow-hop and throw drill should be practiced diligently. However, there are instances when time will not permit the crow-hop before the fielder makes the throw. Therefore, he should be able to make the play without the crow-hop when necessity demands it.

Procedure

A. With infielders in position, the coach hits ground balls to a specific fielder, who fields the ball correctly with his feet spread, left foot slightly forward, and knees bent. (Reverse the foot position for left handed player.) The player then begins to straighten up, keeping his feet in the same position, with his weight evenly distributed. He springs his weight forward, hopping to and landing on his right foot. As he throws overhanded, the infielder steps forward with his left foot. Just after he releases the ball his right foot strikes the ground in a follow-through motion.

Hit 25-50 balls to each infielder.

B. Place outfielders in position. As the coach hits balls to the out-fielders, the right handed fielder fields the ball as described above, but as he comes up he shifts his weight to the left foot, steps forward on his right, and lands on his right foot. As the right foot comes down, the fielder hops on it and steps forward with his left as he throws. Immedi-ately after the release of the ball, the right foot hits the ground on the follow-through.

If the ball is caught in the air and on the move, the fielder catches the ball in stride just as his right foot hits the ground, hops on his right foot, and throws, with the left foot hitting the ground on the stride. After the ball is released, the right leg comes on through in the usual follow-through.

Hit 25-30 balls to each fielder.

C. Pitchers should use the same procedure as the outfielders and include a step before the crow-hop. For left-handers, in the above posi-tion, the processes must be reversed, as mentioned before.

It should be emphasized that on a close play the fielder will have to forget the crow-hop and throw the ball in the best manner possible.

35. Pepper Games

(Note Condition Drill 29.)

36. Multiple Ball Drill

Purpose

To orient the fielders so they can throw without first looking. Also, to give the fielders additional work.

Procedure

This drill is performed with a full team on the field. Each fielder has a hitter to hit balls to him, and each hitter has a pick-up man to catch the ball thrown to him by the fielder. Each hitter has from five to eight balls, so that he can hit rapid fire to the fielder. The fielder fields the ball and tosses it to the pick-up man. However, if the fielder misses the ball, he lets it go because the hitter will continue to hit to him without waiting for the fielder to retrieve a missed ball.

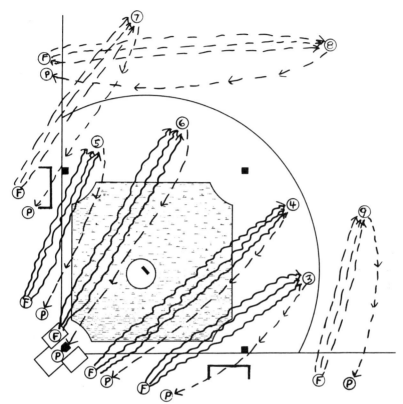

DRILL NO. 36: Multiple Ball

After five minutes of this, the batter hitting to the first baseman stops, and the first baseman takes first to receive balls thrown from the third baseman. The third baseman now takes rapid-fire ground balls and throws to the first baseman, who returns the ball to the hitter's pick-up man. Continue this for five minutes, repeat for the shortstop, then for the second baseman. Players not taking part in this phase of the drill will continue fielding rapid fire in their positions. The drill then moves to the third baseman, who throws to the second baseman, who makes the double play, all rapid fire. Continue this phase of the drill for five minutes, and repeat first with the shortstop, then the second baseman.

By the time the drill has been passed around the infield, the outfielders should have their arms loose, and the drill can be completed by having them throw to the bases and to the cut-off men.

37. Pop Flies with All Players in Position

Purpose

To acquaint all players with the proper way to handle pop flies.

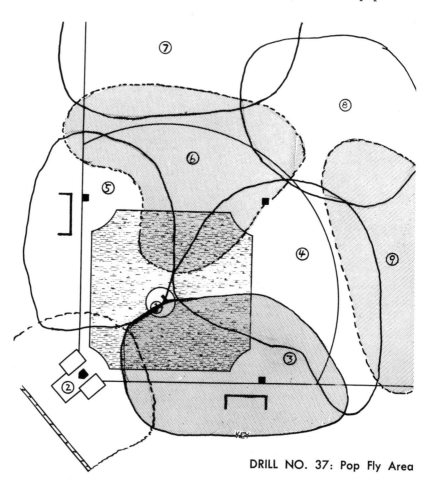

DRILL NO. 37: Pop Fly Area

Procedure

This drill should be practiced as much as possible on three types of days—windy, cloudy, and sunny. A new ball should be used so that players will be acquainted with pop flies in a game-like situation.

In order to make the situation realistic, all players should be in their respective positions, with the catcher in full gear. First, the coach should hit a few pop flies near the mound and home plate. This gives infielders and catchers an opportunity to play this type of ball. Flies near the mound provide the pitcher with practice in getting out of the way of the infielders playing the ball, and helping the infielders by using his voice. Flies should also be hit around and behind first base so that the first baseman and second baseman can get practice in fielding pop flies. When pop flies are directly behind the first baseman, they belong to the second baseman. This is also true for third base where the short-stop plays pop flies behind the third baseman.

The coach then hits those tough pop flies between the infield and the outfield. In calling for these balls the only person to yell (loud and clear) is the outfielder. Every ball belongs to the infielder until the outfielder yells him off it. The infielder merely moves back under the ball while waving his hands up high if he can catch it. He listens for the outfielder to say, "I got it!" several times, or, "Take it!" several times. He never calls a name. If the outfielder says, "I got it!" the infielder pulls out of the way and yells, "Take it!" several times.

A point should be emphasized here. Fly balls between outfielders are run by the centerfielder. If both outfielders yell at the same time, the centerfielder takes the ball, and the other outfielder drops back yelling, "Take it! Take it! Take it!"

38. Hit-and-Run Base Running

Purpose

To practice the hit-and-run and base running. This drill also provides numerous opportunities for practice of cut-off plays.

Procedure

With base coaches and the defensive team in position, place a runner on first base. A batter gives the hit-and-run sign to the runner, who acknowledges it. Although the pitcher tries to get the ball over the plate and mixes up his pitches, he does not try to strike out the batter. The batter must hit the ball, regardless of the pitch, even if he must throw his bat at the ball, so that he may protect the runner. The batter tries to hit behind the runner or to the opposite field. A left handed hitter tries to hit through the hole left by a shortstop covering second.

There should always be a man on first base. If the runner at first advances to second or third, he should stay there. The hitter takes first regardless of whether he is safe or out. Each player on the team should get his chance at bat.

The runner on a hit-and-run breaks on the pitch and *looks up at the hitter* as soon as he hears the crack of the bat. He must know if the ball is a fly ball or ground ball, to avoid being doubled off on a fly ball.

If a catcher is used, he should make every effort to protect his throwing hand since hit-and-run plays generally produce many foul-tipped balls.

39. Cut-Off Plays

Purpose

The purpose of this drill is to acquaint the entire team with all possible relay and cut-off plays in a game. It is also to determine the best possible way to make cut-off plays according to the abilities of the team, and to improve upon these abilities.

The ideal cut-off situation has every base covered and key bases backed up on every play. Hit balls and thrown balls are backed up whenever possible. The cut-off man can fake the cut-off, thus holding the other runners to their bases or making them hesitate enough for an alternate play in case they advance.

On every fair ball, and often on foul fly balls, all nine men have actual or possible participation in the play.

Perfect cut-off plays require perfect players; therefore, the ideal cut-off for one team may not be ideal for another, but it may be the best possible to fit a particular team's ability.

Note Drill Nos. 138-D, 154-E, 164.

Procedure

Put the entire defensive team on the field, and set up the following situations by calling the play before you (the coach) hit the ball. Where runners are indicated, use them to make the situations real.

Stress that the first throw from the outfielder to the relay man is a short, snappy throw, shoulder high on the glove side. The infielder makes the long, hard throw at the cut-off man's head. Have every throw completely backed up. Pay particular attention to pitchers.

Play situations:

1. Nobody on, single to right.
2. Nobody on, single to center.
3. Nobody on, single to left.
4. Man on first, single to right.
5. Man on first, single to center.
6. Man on first, single to left.
7. Men on first and second, single to right.
8. Men on first and second, single to center.
9. Men on first and second, single to left.
10. Nobody on, extra base hit to right.
11. Nobody on, extra base hit to center.
12. Nobody on, extra base hit to left.
13. Man on first, extra base hit to right.
14. Man on first, extra base hit to center.
15. Man on first, extra base hit to left.
16. Men on first and second, extra base hit to right.
17. Men on first and second, extra base hit to center.
18. Men on first and second, extra base hit to left.

40. Special Drills for Cut-Off Play Procedure

(Note Drills: Catcher—110; First Base—129-C,D, 135; Second Base—138-D; Shortstop—154-E, 164; Third Base—172-D.)

41. Bunt Defense

Purpose

The purpose of this drill is to acquaint the team with all possible bunting situations and to develop competency in defense against the bunts.

Procedure

Place the entire defensive team on the field and use base runners for bunting plays. Have the pitcher throw a ball to the catcher. The coach rolls a different ball to the area for the bunt. Set up all bunting

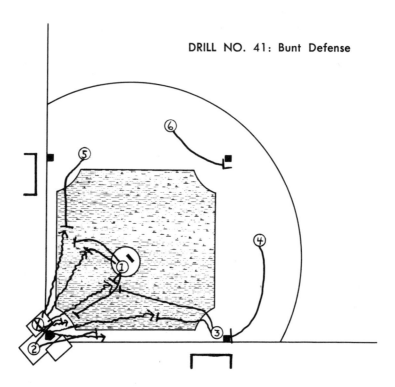

DRILL NO. 41: Bunt Defense

situations, calling the play for the ball which is put into play. In all bunting situations, in order to predetermine whether the batter might be bunting, the pitcher assumes his set stance. Then, he either backs off the rubber or throws to first. In either case the batter, if bunting, may make some move to tip off the bunt. (Note Drills: Shortstop—156; Third Base—168-169; First Base—130-C, 133; Second Base—141; Catcher—113, 115-C; Outfield—187.

42. General Pick-Off Plays

Purpose

To teach the players how to make a pick-off play; not necessarily to pick a runner off, but to show it to the opposition to keep them honest.

Procedure

This drill is worked best by putting all players in their respective positions. Runners should be placed in desired positions for the pick-off play. When the pick-off is attempted, all players must assume their proper positions for backing up the play. If a runner is picked off, let the play continue until he is safe or out.

Be sure that the pitcher and the player making the pick-off use the signs they would use in the game to let each other know that a pick-off is to be attempted. It would be wise to cue the other players in on the signs, so that they can ready themselves to back up the play.

In picking a runner off second base, when the pitcher makes the throw, two methods are used—the *daylight* and the *count* methods.

1. Daylight method: The pitcher takes his stretch, looks toward second, looks back at home and throws to the base after he sees daylight between his shortstop and the runner as the shortstop breaks for the bag.
2. Count method: The pitcher looks at the runner, looks toward the plate, counts 1-2, and throws to second on 3. The short-stop breaks for second as soon as the pitcher turns his head toward home.

The catcher's pick-off play should also be explained here. This play can be used with a runner on any base. The pitcher checks his runners, then delivers his pitch, which should be a pitch-out. When the ball is 12-15 feet in front of the plate, the player to whom the ball will be thrown breaks toward the base and waits for the throw from the catcher.

(For more about pick-offs, see Pitching Drills 95; Second Baseman—150; Shortstop—161; Third Baseman—173.)

43. One Pitch—Six Outs

Purpose

To improve fielding when there are numerous base runners. It sets up natural play situations and should be used during the first and second weeks of practice out-of-doors.

Procedure

Except for the following, baseball rules are in effect:

a. The pitcher is on the offensive side; that is, he throws the batter a good ball to hit.

b. There are six outs instead of three for the team at bat.

c. Only one pitch is thrown to each batter. He is out if he takes the pitch without swinging, fouls it, or is put out by a defensive player. He is safe on a hit or an error. The defensive player making the play calls the outs and safes.

44. Two Pitch—Six Outs

This game is utilized at the beginning of the third week of practice, and should be played occasionally between regular games. It speeds up the number of innings, thus allowing more play in game-type situations.

Two pitch is played exactly as one pitch, except that the hitter does not have to swing at the first pitch if he does not like it. If he takes it, he must swing at the second pitch, or he will be called out. There is an opportunity to get a better ball to hit with two pitches.

45. Full Count—Six Outs

This team drill is played with baseball rules except for two differences. The defensive players act as umpires. The catcher calls balls and strikes; the infielders call outs and safes at the bases, and the outfielders call foul balls deep down the foul line. It gives the players game-like conditions.

The other important difference is that the team at bat gets six outs each inning before being retired. By allowing the offensive team six outs, more innings can be played; pitchers do not have to warm up as often, and both teams get more fielding chances and times at bat. The pitchers have more opportunities to pitch with men on base, and the infield gets more opportunities to make the important double play.

CHAPTER 4

BATTING DRILLS

Batting is one of the most important activities of any practice day and should take more time than any other one activity. If a player has strength and works hard enough he can improve his hitting. There are very few hitters who cannot be helped. These drills are designed to develop the individual in team practice and on his own time. During the off-season numerous drills may improve a hitter, but when the season begins, many, many swings at a ball are needed. Batting practice means exactly what it says. Pitchers must let the batter hit the ball in order to improve his timing and bolster his confidence.

One of the most important assets of a batter is knowing what to do when he is at bat. If he cannot hit he should learn to think. These drills should help mentally as well as physically.

46. Check-List for Proper Execution—Bat Grip

(Note Screening Candidate Drill No. 207.)

Proper grip of the bat is probably one of the most overlooked procedures in hitting. When gripping the bat, the middle knuckles of both hands line up or are nearly lined up. The middle knuckles of the top hand can be lined up between the middle knuckles and those knuckles at the base of the fingers on the bottom hand.

The bat in the top hand (right hand for right handed hitters) is held slightly diagonally and gripped with the fingers. The pressure of the bat when hitting the ball is more against the palm of the hand just under the knuckle, at the base of the index finger, rather than in the cushion area between the thumb and index finger. It is practically the same grip used on a tennis racquet or golf club.

The index fingers are completely relaxed and held off the bat or very lightly against the bat. The grip prior to the swing is relaxed and is mostly with the thumb and other three fingers. When the swing is made, all fingers grip the bat firmly.

47. Ball Toss Fungo Batting

Purpose

To teach batters to extend their arms as the bat makes contact with the ball.

Procedure

Needed for this drill are the following: a protective screen, two bats, an ample supply of baseballs, and two players.

The screen is set up about 10 feet from the batter. The other player, the feeder, kneels behind the screen and tosses balls around its corner in such a way that they will enter the strike zone of the batter, who hits the balls tossed to him.

A. For the first 25-30 balls tossed to him, the batter should use a 35-inch bat with a medium-sized handle. This bat should weigh about 50 ounces. Since the batter's arms should be fully extended when the bat contacts the ball, this big, heavy bat will naturally pull his arms away from his body when he swings. The heavy bat will also help to develop the hitter's arms, forearms, and wrists. (Note Gimmick No. 223.)

B. For the next 25-30 tossed balls, the hitter should use his regular bat. However, the batter should continue to concentrate on extending his arms as the bat contacts the ball. This is a must for good hitting. (Note Illustration No. 7.)

48. Swing Strengthener

(Note Gimmick Nos. 220-223.)

49. Dry Swing Team Batting

Purpose

The development of the batter's ability to master different swings to meet a variety of pitchers. It is especially valuable when no batting cage is available.

Procedure

Team members line up in a straight line with bats in hand, leaving sufficient room between batters for each to take a full swing without danger of hitting each other or each other's bats.

The coach stands behind the batters and calls hypothetical pitches out loud to the batters, such as "inside fast ball," "low outside curve," and "high fast ball." On the coach's command, "Ready, swing," each batter swings at the imaginary ball as though the pitch were thrown to him. Fifty to sixty swings should be sufficient. The coach should remember to call every possible pitch the team might face.

50. Mirror Swing

This drill is designed to permit the batter to see his swing, check various phases of it, and by so doing, to improve his ability to swing at his maximum capacity.

Procedure

The player stands in front of the mirror, facing it, and takes several practice swings, making them as natural as possible. He pays particular attention to wrist roll, level swing, eye movement, stride, arm, and head movement. However, he should watch only one thing at a time. In this manner he tries to develop his swing until he has reached his maximum ability.

51. Hanging Target Swing

Purpose

Designed to help the player in swinging a bat, this drill should also assist him in keeping his head still and eyes on the ball while swinging. The drill should improve his ability to hit pitches at different heights.

Procedure

A. *Stuffed Stocking on String:*

The target is a rag- or paper-filled stocking suspended by a string from the ceiling of a room. It is best to have several of these at different heights, so that players can get practice hitting at balls of various heights, inside and outside.

The player should have two bats of his own model, and one of these should be filled with lead in the large end. First, the player should swing the leaded bat, then the regular bat. He should swing as many times as he can. Fifty to 100 swings is not too much for off-season work.

An ideal place for a ball player to set up this drill is in a garage or cellar.

B. *Stuffed Stocking:*

Stuff a stocking and tape it loosely. This object can be hit indoors without damaging anything. It is excellent for indoor swings and getting your eye on the ball.

52. Baseball Bat Figure Eight

Purpose

Designed to loosen up the wrists, arms and shoulders, this drill also develops the muscles necessary for power hitting.

Procedure

1. Take a bat in one hand by grasping it near the knob at the end of the handle and extend it horizontally to one side. Use the bat as you would an Indian Club, making a figure eight

ILLUS. NO. 8

44

ILLUS. NO. 9

with it. Start with a small figure eight and increase to a large windmill figure eight. Then repeat with the other hand. Repeat both drills for several minutes. (Note Illustration No. 8, page 44)

2. Now, put the bat in both hands in front of the body and begin a figure eight movement. Continue for several minutes. (Note Illustration No. 9, page 45)

53. Shadow Drill

Purpose

To teach players to swing at the ball without moving their heads forward or downward.

The hitter stands with his back to the sun so that his shadow is cast on the ground in front of him. A spot is made on the ground where the shadow of his head is cast. Taking his normal swing with the bat, the player watches his shadow to see whether it moves. Although no movement is desirable, a small amount is not bad. The hitter continues to swing until he can swing normally with little or no movement of his head shadow.

The coach can stand on the head shadow in order to note any movement.

54. Isometric Bat Drill

Purpose

To increase and develop the hitting power of the batter's swing, as the term *isometric* may indicate. The drill should be practiced before and after workouts, and it should be continued during winter months.

Procedure

Desired results will be obtained only when the exercises described here are executed at maximum effort.

With a bat in his hands the hitter addresses a solidly placed pole as he would face home plate when he is ready to hit.

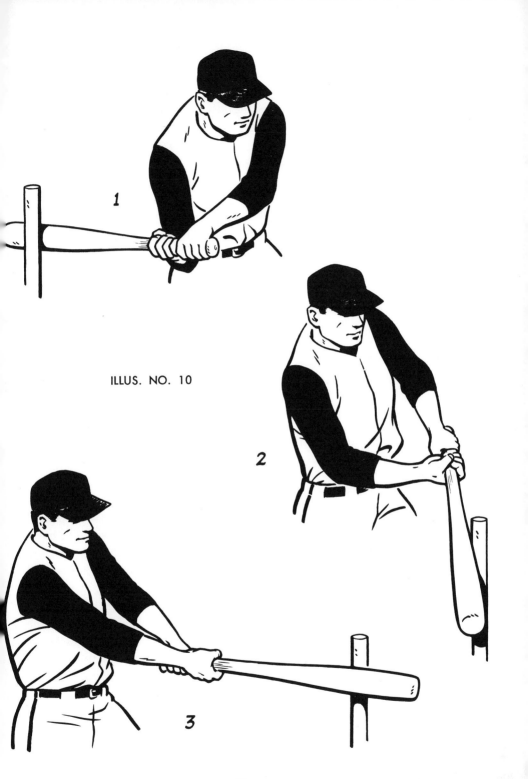

1

ILLUS. NO. 10

2

3

a. First position: Standing one step in front of the pole, the batter places the bat against the pole simulating a stopped swing at its very beginning. He then tries to *pull* the bat through the pole for a six-second count. (Note Illustration No. 10, Figure 1, page 47.)

b. Second position: In this position, the batter stands even with the pole, places his bat against it as though it were in mid-swing position, and presses against the pole at maximum effort for six seconds. (Note Illustration No. 10, Figure 2.)

c. Third position: Finally, the player assumes a stance one step behind the pole, places the bat against it in a three-quarter swing position, and pushes with full effort against the pole for six seconds. (Note Illustration No. 10, Figure 3.)

55. Hip Rotation Drill

Purpose

To teach the hitter hip rotation so that it becomes natural—a part of his complete movement in swinging at a pitched ball.

Procedure

The batter assumes a normal batting stance. He places a bat behind him, horizontal to the ground, and locks it in position with the inner elbows. After the bat is in position, he turns his head and eyes and focuses on an object in the direction from which the pitch would come.

At this point he starts rotating his hip: right-left, right-left, as far as possible, keeping his head and eyes level and looking at the object selected as the pitcher. He does this 25 times in succession.

Next, taking the bat in his hands and assuming a batting stance, he incorporates a swing of the bat with the hip rotations, but he keeps his feet still. There should be 25 of these movements.

Finally, he takes 25 swings of the bat with good hip rotation and a normal batting stride.

56. Bat Throwing Drill

Purpose

This drill is designed to improve the player's ability to literally throw the bat at the ball, so that he will get more power into his swing. The drill should help the hitter to hit the long ball.

Procedure

The player takes 10-15 bats into the outfield for use in practicing the bat throwing. He must be sure that no one is on the field and that bats will not hit an object such as a post or fence.

The batter takes a normal stance and loose grip on the bat. In order to get the best action in the swing of the bat he should extend his arms and snap his wrists. After the wrists are snapped, the batter should release the bat so that it will fly into the field in the direction of an imaginary pitcher.

This drill can be practiced daily.

57. Breaking from Home

Purpose

To improve the hitters' technique and speed in breaking from home as soon as his swing is completed.

Procedure

Line the team up near home plate, but caution your players to stay away from the area of a possible flying bat. As soon as a hitter finishes his swing, the next batter steps up to hit. Five or six rounds of this should be ample for one day of practice. Three or four days' practice of this drill should be sufficient during the early season.

The hitter takes his regular batting stance and breaks for first base at the crack of the bat on any hit ball—foul or fair. Time the runner to a mark half way to first base. A right handed hitter should strive for 2.5 seconds, a lefty should make it in two seconds.

The coach should make every effort to get hitters to react quickly and break toward first as soon as the bat cracks. Some players would like to pause momentarily and admire their hit.

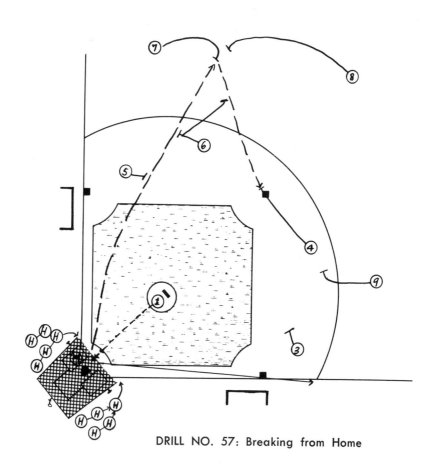

DRILL NO. 57: Breaking from Home

58. Batting "Tee" Drill

(Note Gimmick No. 212.)

59. Pepper Games

(Note Conditioner Drill No. 29.)

60. Developing a Poor Hitter

Purpose

The purpose of these drills is to develop the poor hitter. Since the inability to hit well usually is due to a combination of factors, all or some of the following drills should be used, many of them under the direction of the coach. The most common faults are taking the eye off the ball and overstriding.

No. 46. Check-List for Proper Execution—Bat Grip
No. 47. Ball Toss Fungo Hitting
No. 50. Mirror Swing
No. 53. Shadow Swing
No. 56. Bat Throwing
No. 61. Place Hitting and Hit-and-Run Drill
No. 217. Stuffed Stocking
No. 220. Ball on Swinging Rope
No. 221. Hitting Tire
No. 222. Lead Bat
No. 223. Fifty-Ounce Bat

61. Place Hitting and Hit-and-Run Drill

Purpose

Although the principal purpose of this drill is to help the batter to come out of a slump due to some fault, such as overstriding or not keeping his eye on the ball, it is excellent as a drill for hit-and-run practice.

Procedure

In his effort to hit to the opposite field, the hitter may choose one or both of the following methods:

a. He may swing late and hit the ball behind or over the plate, rather than in front of it, thus causing it to go to the opposite field.

b. The batter may step back from the plate (not toward the catcher) with his back foot, and then step in toward the pitch with his front foot, again meeting the ball over or behind the plate and hitting to the opposite field.

The coach should get the batter to try both methods, still maintaining as nearly as possible his natural swing, stride, and batting position. This should be practiced over and over until some progress is made.

62. Team Batting Practice

Purpose

To have an organized system for holding batting practice.

Procedure

A. *Early Season.* During the first few days the work should be on fundamentals, but no hard swings should be taken. The batters should be trying to get their eyes on the ball and a correct roll of the wrist in the swing. Each player should take two bunts—one to first base area and one to the third base area, then five or six swings. After that they should rotate so that each player bats three or four times during the practice session, which should last for one hour. Pitchers should be included in this early batting practice.

B. *During Season.* During the season each player should take one bunt and four swings, then rotate so that each player gets in as many turns at bat as possible, still limiting the session to one hour. Pitchers scheduled to pitch the next day can be included in this drill.

If time does not permit a full round of four swings for the last turn, the number of swings should be cut. Perhaps a hit-and-run swing can be used here, with each player getting several rounds.

Outfielders can start the batting practice, infielders next, and catchers next. They should rotate daily, thus cutting down arguments. Catchers run the practice by telling each hitter how many swings he has left.

CHAPTER 5

BUNTING DRILLS

Bunting need not be a lost art; it merely takes time and work. The bunter must visualize the top half of the ball meeting the bottom half of the head of the bat, with the bat angled so as to bunt the ball near a foul line or in the area desired. He must also realize that being up in the front part of the batter's box gives him a better opportunity to bunt the ball fair.

These drills are designed to teach angle of bunting, area of bunting, and the art of bunting. Some bunting can be practiced on the sidelines with other players. Pitchers in particular should learn to bunt. A sacrifice in the early innings may result in a run which will keep the pitcher in the game during the late innings. A poor bunter will often be removed for a pinch-hitter.

63. Check-List for Proper Execution

(Note Screening Candidates Drill No. 207.)

64. Bunting Bat to Be Used for All Bunting Drills

(Note Gimmick No. 219.)

65. Position of Feet and Body

Purpose

To develop in the players the habit of using the proper footsteps in the sacrifice bunt.

Procedure

(Positions and steps described below are for the right handed batter; those for left handed batters are reversed.)

A. *Square around.* (Note Illustration No. 11, page 55.)

When the pitcher's striding leg comes up off the ground, the batter acts as though he intends to swing. Then, when the pitcher's striding foot strikes the ground, the batter should square around.

His left foot steps away from the plate, and his right foot comes up parallel with his left, and he is facing the pitcher. The bunter's body is slightly crouched and his elbows are close to the body, relaxed. He has the bat held in front of him parallel to the ground. The bat is angled and gripped as described in Drill No. 66.

B. *Pivot in tracks.* (Note Illustration No. 12, page 56.)

The bat position for the pivot-in-tracks is the same as in the square-around-bunt position.

The batter remains in his tracks and on the balls of his feet. He pivots his hips, and his feet point toward the pitcher. His body faces the pitcher, and he uses the same grip, angle, and bat position as in Drill No. 66.

66. Angle of Bat Drill

Purpose

To teach the bunter the proper angle to hold the bat in order to execute the perfect bunt.

Procedure

Have each bunter take a turn at the plate and let him practice bunting until he appears to understand the proper angle to hold the bat.

The bat may be gripped by moving the top hand up near the trade mark and bottom hand about four inches from the handle. (Note Illustration No. 13, Figure 1.) Or, it may be gripped by moving

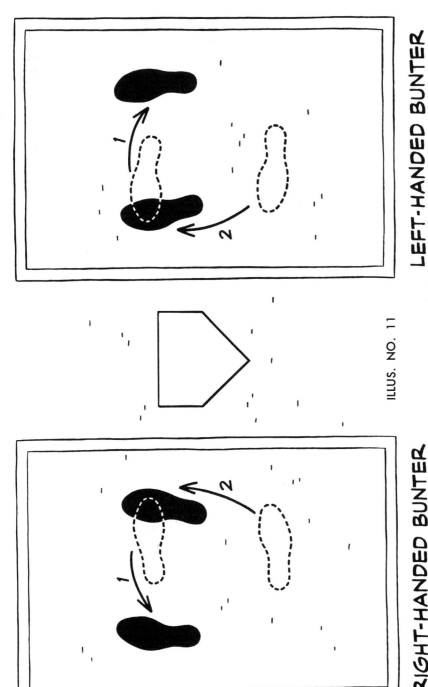

LEFT-HANDED BUNTER

RIGHT-HANDED BUNTER

ILLUS. NO. 11

55

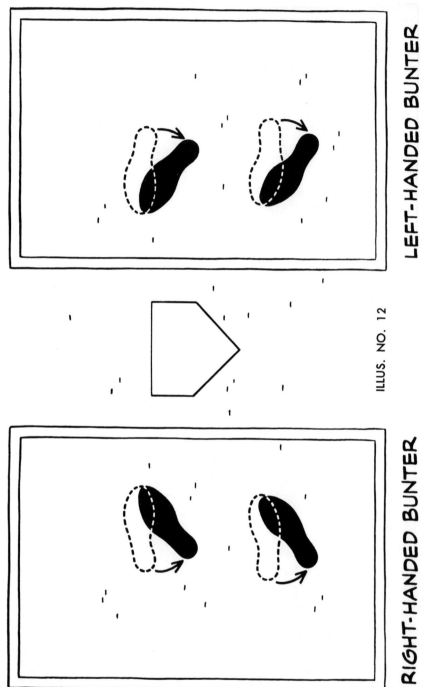

LEFT-HANDED BUNTER

RIGHT-HANDED BUNTER

ILLUS. NO. 12

both hands up, holding the bat with the top hand about two inches from the trade mark. (Note Illustration No. 13, Figure No. 2, page 58.)

In the spread grip, the bottom hand holds the bat loosely and curls around the handle. The top hand cups the bat without curling the fingers around it. The grip is mostly with the thumb, index finger, and middle finger. The other fingers are tucked in and under the bat.

The two-hands-together grip has both hands gripped firmly but not tightly around the bat.

In all cases, hold the bat parallel to the ground, chest high and covering the plate, with elbows near the body. Let the ball contact the bat with the top half of the ball striking the bottom half of the "meat" of the bat.

A. *Right handed hitter*
1. To first base area
   Extend left arm and bend right arm. Get on top of the ball. (Note Illustration No. 14, page 59.)
2. To third base area
   Point the head of the bat at the first baseman, leaving the right arm extended and the left arm crooked. (Note Illustration No. 15, page 60.)

B. *Left handed hitter*
1. To first base area
   Leaving the left arm extended and the right arm crooked, point the head of the bat at the third baseman. (Note Illustration No. 16, page 61.)
2. To third base area
   Point the handle of the bat at the first baseman, with the right arm extended slightly and the left arm crooked. (Note Illustration No. 17, page 62.)

67. Sacrifice Bunting to First Base Area

Purpose

To develop bunting skills of players until they can bunt accurately into the first base area, thus taking advantage of a weak-fielding first baseman. This ability is also valuable when the third baseman is crowding the batter and when the first baseman is right handed.

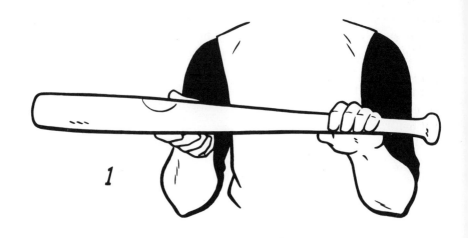

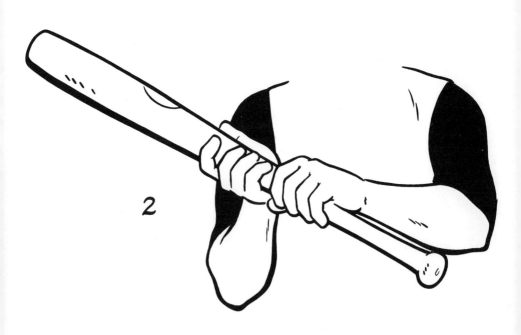

ILLUS. NO. 13

PIVOT IN TRACKS

SQUARE AROUND

ILLUS. NO. 14

PIVOT IN TRACKS   SQUARE AROUND

ILLUS. NO. 15

60

PIVOT IN TRACKS   SQUARE AROUND

ILLUS. NO. 16

SQUARE AROUND

ILLUS. NO. 17

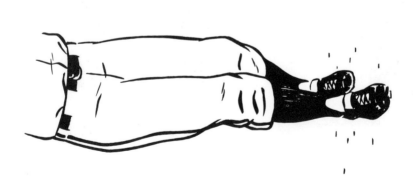

PIVOT IN TRACKS

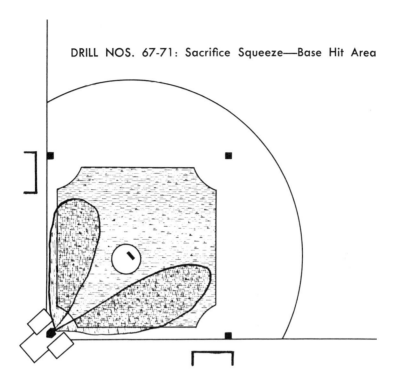

DRILL NOS. 67-71: Sacrifice Squeeze—Base Hit Area

Procedure

A. Right handed hitter: practice drill No. 66, A-1. (Illustration No. 14)

B. Left handed hitter: practice drill No. 66, B-1. (Illustration No. 16)

Practice drill until desired proficiency by hitters is attained.

68. Sacrifice Bunt to Third Base Area

Purpose

To develop the player's ability to bunt accurately and consistently into the third base area. Players bunt only strikes. A sacrifice bunt means exactly what it says. The bunter must sacrifice himself to make a good bunt.

Procedure

Give every player an opportunity to bunt 10 times in this drill.

1. Use position of feet and body as described in Drill No. 65.
2. Right handed batters:
    a. Point head of bat toward first base. This gives the bat the proper angle to bunt the ball toward third base.
    b. The left arm with bent elbow is held near the body.
    c. The right arm is extended, but bent slightly to give a little as the bat contacts the ball.
    d. The bat should be held chest high with the head of the bat covering the plate.
    e. Get on top of the ball. (Illustration No. 15)
3. Left handed batters:
    a. Right arm is extended with a slight bend in the elbow and the *handle* of the bat points toward first base.
    b. The left arm with bent elbow is kept close to the body.
    c. The bat is held chest high with the head of the bat covering the plate.
    d. Get on top of the ball. (Illustration No. 17)

69. Bunt for a Base Hit—First Base Area

Purpose

To teach batters the proper way to bunt for a base hit in the first base area.

Procedure

Put the infield in position with a pitcher on the mound and a catcher behind the plate.

A. *Right handed batter: the "push" bunt.* The batter stands at the plate, decoying a possible swing at the ball. As the pitcher cocks his arm in his delivery, the batter rotates his hips to the rear as if to take a full swing. When the ball is released by the pitcher, the batter takes a cross-over step, stepping with his right foot toward the second baseman. At the same time he is stepping, he also sets the angle of the bat with the end of the handle pointing halfway between third base and home plate. The batter must meet the ball before the right foot hits the ground. Holding the bat in this position, he "pushes" the ball past the pitcher and directly at the second baseman.

B. *Left handed batter: the "drag" bunt.* The batter stands at the plate, decoying a possible swing. As the pitcher cocks his arm in his delivery motion, the batter rotates his hips to the rear as though he would take a full swing. When the pitcher releases the ball the batter takes a cross-over step, stepping with his left foot over his right foot. At the same time he is stepping, he also sets the angle of the bat so that the big end points halfway between third base and home plate. The batter should meet the ball before his left foot hits the ground. Holding the bat in the bunting position, the hitter "drags" the ball down the first base line with him, toward the second baseman, past the pitcher.

70. Bunt for a Base Hit to the Third Base Area

Purpose

To develop hitters' ability to bunt safely to the third base area.

Procedure

When bunting for a base hit, the batter should bunt the ball as close to the foul line as possible. If the ball stays fair along the foul line, the player's chances of reaching first base safely are much better than they would be if he bunted the ball into the middle of the infield. If the ball should roll foul, the hitter has another chance.

A. *Right handed hitter.* The hitter takes his normal batting stance. As the pitcher releases the ball the hitter rotates the upper part of his body clockwise and draws his bat back simulating a swing. When the ball is about 20 feet from the plate the hitter sets his feet and bat into position.

He assumes this position by stepping one stride backward with his right foot; that is, to the left of home plate. As this movement is made, the weight is shifted to the left foot. However, once the feet are set, the weight is shifted again to the right foot.

The bat is set into position by sliding both hands up the handle from six to twelve inches. The head of the bat points toward first base, and the handle of the bat is slid between the hitter's right side and his right elbow. It is parallel to the ground and slightly above the right hip.

Some hitters like to have their hands separated when bunting. If this is the case, the right hand should slide about 10 inches while the left hand slides about six inches toward the head of the bat.

B. Another method of bunting for a hit. Follow the same procedure as "A" above for the feet and body, except that the hands and bat are held in front of the body toward the pitcher. The hands are held either together or spread. The bat meets the ball in front of the plate at an angle, with the head of the bat pointed toward first base. The right foot steps toward the ball as the ball meets the bat.

C. Left handed hitter. The left handed hitter follows the same procedure as the right handed player until the ball is about 20 feet away, except that his body rotates counterclockwise.

He sets his feet in position by crossing the left foot over the right toward first base when contacting the ball. In order to get the bat into position the left-hander slides his left hand up the handle of the bat six to twelve inches. The handle of the bat is pointed toward first base when the bunt is being made, and the handle should be held away from the body. The hands can be spread or held together.

71. Bunt for a Squeeze

Purpose

To develop the bunting skills of players to the extent that they can lay down a bunt when needed with such accuracy that it will be away from the pitcher.

Procedure

A. Safety squeeze: Set up a game-like situation with defense in position and a runner on third. The pitcher takes a wind-up or a set stance, then throws to batter. The runner at third advances when the bunted ball is on the ground. He returns to third base on a missed ball or a pop bunt.

This is similar to a sacrifice bunt (Drill No. 68), but the main thing is to bunt the ball away from the pitcher. He bunts only strikes.

B. Suicide squeeze: Set up the same situation as in the safety squeeze. The batter gives the runner the sign, and the runner acknowledges it. The batter *must* bunt the ball even if it is thrown at him, for this will protect the runner coming home from third base.

The ball is bunted anywhere on the ground, but the runner does not break for home until the pitcher strides and his foot hits the ground, just as his throwing arm and hand are by his head, in a vertical position. The runner breaks at that time, *but never before.*

Pitchers and weak hitters should do a lot of bunting of this type; however, all players should have their turns.

72. Fake Bunt and Hit

Purpose

The drill is designed to help players develop the ability to fake a bunt in a bunt situation, but where the infield is in too far for safe bunting, then swing instead of bunt.

Procedure

The batter squares around to bunt or pivots in his tracks, as in Drill No. 65, then fakes a bunt. The hands are together, but fairly high on the bat. As the pitcher releases the ball, the batter rotates his hips slightly toward the catcher and takes a short swing, stepping with his front foot toward the ball as he swings. The batter should never attempt to take a full swing, because this may make him pop up or miss the ball.

Pitching is often said to be 75 percent of the game. With this in mind, pitchers must work hard to get in shape. Their arm is only as good as their legs. Pitchers do considerably more running than other players. They must gradually get their arms ready for the season, but should begin throwing a few hard ones early in the season. They should spin the ball for the curve ball the first day, but should not break it off for a fast curve. The following drills are designed for good conditioning and mastery of the mound.

CHAPTER 6

PITCHING DRILLS

73. Check-List for Proper Execution

(Note Screening Candidates Drill No. 207.)

74. Spot Control Pitching Drill

Purpose

To teach pitchers to throw at specific targets, and to develop their control so that they can hit their targets.

Procedure

Place the pitcher on the mound and the catcher in his position behind the plate, or have them assume the proper distance for pitching along the side

ILLUS. NO. 18

lines. The pitcher then throws at his catcher's left and right shoulders, left and right knees, at his chest, and finally at his glove. (Note Illustration No. 18.)

The catcher keeps track of the pitcher's hits and misses.

75. String Target (Note Gimmick No. 229.)

76. Control Practice in Gym

Purpose

To help pitchers in developing better control and to give them work on control prior to outdoor practice.

Procedure

A. *String Target.* The pitcher throws through strings to the catcher, who should wear a mask for protection. The catcher keeps count of the strikes and number of pitches. (Note Gimmick No. 229.)

B. *Tape Target.* The pitcher throws at a tape target located on a wall or taped to a hanging mat. The pitcher keeps track of the number of pitches and strikes. (Note Gimmick No. 230.)

In either drill, the pitcher should throw 15 consecutive strikes before quitting.

77. Pitcher Control Drill

Purpose

To help the pitcher learn the strike zone and to be able to hit it.

Procedure

Put a pitcher on the mound, a catcher behind the plate and a batter in the batter's box. Have the pitcher throw his different pitches to the catcher, who calls the pitches and teams with the batter in acting as umpire. The batter does not swing at the pitches. In most cases the batter and the catcher will agree on the pitch; however, if they disagree, the pitch probably is in a very good location.

Alternate between left handed and right handed hitters.

A. Have the catcher call 10 pitches, while the pitcher and the batter discuss the calls.

B. Have the batter call 10 pitches, while the catcher and pitcher discuss the calls.

C. Have the pitcher call 10 pitches, while the catcher and the batter discuss the calls.

After each pitcher is warmed up for game condition throwing, have him throw for five minutes. Run this drill several times prior to the season's play.

78. Eye Patch Drill

(Note Gimmick No. 232.)

79. Prevention of Steal Drill

Purpose

To teach the pitcher how to keep the runner on first base from getting a good lead.

Procedure

Put a pitcher on the mound, a catcher behind the plate, and a first baseman and a runner on first base.

A. *Back off.** With a runner on first base, the pitcher comes to a set stance. (Illustration No. 19, Figure No. 2, page 79.) After the runner has taken a lead, the pitcher backs off the rubber and drops his hands. However, he does not move his striding foot. This maneuver, in most cases, will cause the runner to return to the base. Before the runner can get another lead, the pitcher steps on the rubber, gets set, and pitches.

B. *First baseman returns the ball to the pitcher on the rubber.* The pitcher comes set and then throws to first in an attempted pick-off. While throwing to first, the pitcher leaves his pivot foot in contact with the rubber. The first baseman returns the ball to the pitcher, who

* Success of plays A and B depends upon the batter staying in the batter's box.

still has his pivot foot on the rubber. The pitcher becomes set and pitches before the runner takes a lead.

80. Fielding Position on a Batted Ball

Purpose

To help the pitcher learn to field and make the right moves and plays on batted balls.

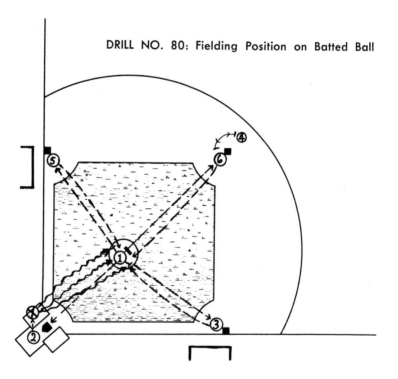

DRILL NO. 80: Fielding Position on Batted Ball

Procedure

The coach is five or six feet away from the batter's box and has a ball and a fungo bat. All players are in position. The pitcher throws a ball to the catcher. As the ball reaches the plate, the coach hits his ball toward the pitcher, who fields it and makes the proper play as described below.

A. *Without base runners:*

The pitcher fields the ball and throws to first base using a crow-hop as described in Drill No. 34, if an emergency throw is not necessary. Both left handed and right handed pitchers pivot counterclockwise on the balls hit directly at them.

B. *With base runners:*

1. With a man on first base, one or no outs, the pitcher fields the ball and fires to second for a force-out or double play. The pitcher must know by a sign given by the shortstop or second baseman, before the pitch, who is covering second base. Signs such as picking up dirt or taking off the glove are usually used. The right handed pitcher pivots counterclockwise, and the left handed pitcher pivots clockwise. In making the throws, both use a crow-hop.

2. When there are runners on first and third and no outs, the pitcher moves the same as above in part 1 of this drill, but he first looks the runner back to third.

3. With men on first and third with one out, follow the same procedure as above.

4. When bases are loaded, one out or no outs, the pitcher fires the ball to home plate for the force-out. However, if there are two outs, he throws to first base.

81. Fielding Drill—Throwing Ball

Purpose

To get the pitcher ready for balls hit through the box and to teach him how to field the ball.

Procedure

Have a pitcher assume a position in front of and near a backstop (with the backstop to his rear). The coach moves approximately 30 to 40 feet away from the pitcher. The coach then throws balls into the dirt to the pitcher's right, left, and directly at him. The pitcher fields the ball with his glove hand only. He keeps his pitching hand away from the ball.

82. Fielding Bunts

Purpose

To develop the pitcher's ability to field bunts properly in all areas and to make necessary throws after fielding them.

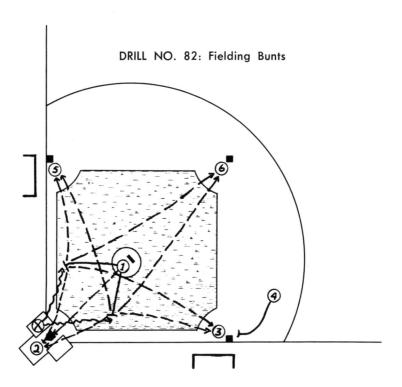

DRILL NO. 82: Fielding Bunts

Procedure

From the rubber, the pitcher delivers a normal pitch to the catcher. As the ball passes the plate, the coach, who is standing in the batter's box with a ball in his hand, rolls a ball to a bunting area. When a pitcher has fielded bunts on both first and third base sides, they rotate so that each pitcher gets an opportunity to field bunts.

In making the different throws, pitchers should use the following procedures:

A. *Throw to First Base:*
   1. Right-handers throw from the position in which the ball is fielded.
   2. Left-handers field the ball, pivot clockwise, and throw when their left foot is set.
B. *Throw to Second Base:* Pitchers should get into position to throw as soon as the ball is picked up.
   1. Right-handers field the ball with the right foot toward home plate and the left toward second base, pivot counterclockwise, and throw.
   2. Left-handers field the ball with left foot toward home and the right foot toward third base, pivot clockwise, and throw.
C. *Throw to Third:* Just the reverse of throwing to first base.
   1. Right-handers pivot counterclockwise and throw as the right foot is set.
   2. Left-handers throw from the position in which the ball is fielded.
D. *Throw to Home Plate:* Give the ball to the catcher firmly, never too hard. It is usually a side arm or underhand toss.
   1. On a force-out, throw the ball to the catcher shoulder high.
   2. In a tag-out play, throw the ball knee high.

83. Covering First Base Drill (Pitchers)

Purpose

To teach the first baseman and pitchers to work together on plays at first base.

Procedure

In this drill, pitchers, a catcher, and a first baseman are used.
A. *No Runners on Base:*
Pitchers line up on the mound, and the first baseman and catcher get into their respective playing positions. As the pitcher throws the ball to the catcher, the coach hits a different ball to the first baseman. The pitcher breaks for first, running in an arc so that when he

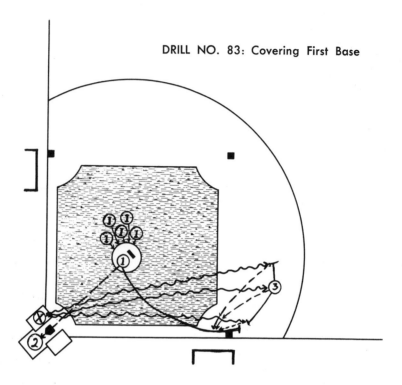

DRILL NO. 83: Covering First Base

is 10 to 15 feet from the bag he is running parallel to the foul line. The first baseman gives the pitcher the ball about three feet in front of the bag. The pitcher's right foot always hits the base, and he then pivots slightly toward the infield to avoid colliding with the base runner.

B. *Runners on Base:*
  1. Right handed pitchers:
    Right handed pitchers make the moves as described above. However, when the pitcher steps away from the base with his left foot, he pivots on it counterclockwise, plants his right foot, and is ready to throw if the runner or runners attempt to take an extra base.
  2. Left handed pitchers:

Same as above, except that as his right foot strikes the bag he pivots clockwise, landing on his left foot away from the bag and throwing from that position.

All pitchers take turns with the drill in different play situations.

84. Wild Pitch—Pass Ball—Covering Home

Purpose

To teach the pitcher to cover home plate on a wild pitch and to call the location of the ball for the catcher.

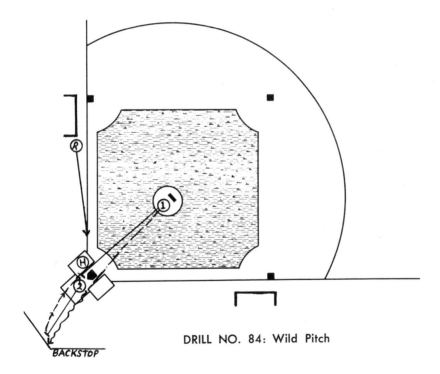

DRILL NO. 84: Wild Pitch

Procedure

A. In order to have the best possible game situation, a batter should be at the plate with a runner on third base.

B. The pitcher on the mound should throw the ball toward the catcher, in the dirt, to his right, to his left, and over his head; that is, he should deliver a variety of wild pitches. The catcher in full gear should block some, but he should permit some to go all the way to the backstop. As the catcher runs for the ball, the pitcher covers home plate. While the pitcher is running in to cover home he should be yelling and pointing to the ball so that the catcher can retrieve it as quickly as possible. Yelling the location of the ball and pointing at it are very essential to the catcher's success in getting the ball as quickly as possible, and all coaches should have their pitchers practice it.

85. Pitcher Rhythm Drill

Purpose

Although all pitchers have rhythm in their delivery, this should help them develop better rhythm.

Procedure

A. The pitcher is on the rubber assuming wind-up stance. (Note Illustration No. 19, Figure No. 1, page 79.) His pivot foot is on the rubber, and the striding foot is behind the rubber. On the count of one, he shifts his weight to the pivot foot, and his arms swing down and back behind the body. (Note Illustration No. 20, Figure No. 1, page 80.) On the count of two, he shifts his weight back to the striding foot, and swings his arms up over the head, with the ball and glove meeting. (Note Illustration No. 20, Figure No. 2.) On the count of three, the striding foot is kicked up and forward; the glove hand is brought down toward the hitter, and the ball hand is brought down behind the body. (Note Illustration No. 20, Figure No. 3.) With the count of four, the striding foot steps toward home plate, toe pointing forward and landing before the heel. The glove hand swings toward the hitter and falls to the side, and the ball is brought toward the catcher. (Note Illustration No. 20, Figure No. 4.) Finishing on the count of five, the pivot foot is brought up even with the striding foot, feet spread, and both hands forward in fielding position. (Note Illustration No. 20, Figure No. 5.)

ILLUS. NO. 19

1. WIND-UP STANCE

2. SET STANCE

ILLUS. NO. 20

B. The pitcher now assumes the set stance. (Note Illustration No. 19, Figure No. 2, page 79.) On the count of one, the striding foot is kicked up and forward, with the glove thrown toward the hitter and the ball brought back behind the body. (Note Illustration No. 20, Figure No. 3.) On the count of two, the striding foot steps toward home plate, toe pointing forward and hitting before the heel. The glove hand swings toward the hitter and falls to the side, and the ball is brought toward the catcher. (Note Illustration No. 20, Figure No. 4.) On the count of three, the pivot step is toward home plate, feet spread and parallel. Both hands are brought forward in fielding position. (Note Illustration No. 20, Figure No. 5.)

86. In-Stride, Snap Throw Drill

Purpose

To help pitchers develop more snap in their wrist and elbow action when throwing. The drill is especially good for pitchers with a big sweeping arm motion.

Procedure

With his foot on the rubber in the set position, and his striding foot at the distance of a normal stride toward home plate (approximately four feet), the pitcher throws the ball from a flat-footed stance, following through with his arm only. His feet remain in the same position.

87. Special Drills for Pitchers

(Note Conditioning Drill Nos. 4, 11-17, 25-26, 28-29.)

88. Bare Hand Drill

Purpose

To prevent pitchers or other ball players from throwing too hard during the first two days of indoor practice, and to aid in the toughening of the hands.

Procedure

Have players pair off and throw to each other in the gym. Insist that no gloves be used for first loosening-up period the first two days. If players are not wearing gloves they will not throw hard enough to develop sore arms.

89. Snap Throw Wrist Developer

(Note Pillow Throw—Gimmick No. 235; Rope for Snap Throwing, Gimmick No. 236.)

90. Rope Pull Arm Strengthener

(Note Gimmick Rope Pull No. 238.)

91. Early Curve Ball Practice

Purpose

To get pitchers' arms ready for throwing curve balls in games.

Procedure

In the first day of practice, after loosening up properly, spin a few easy curves off the fingertips. Do this for no more than five minutes, alternating with straight balls. Repeat this for three or four days. During the fifth day, snap off a few curves. By the second week, pitchers should start throwing curves harder and for a longer time according to the individual, and by the third week they should have the curve ready for game conditions, but in limited amounts.

92. Pitcher Stride Drill

Purpose

To help pitchers develop the correct striding and stepping technique from the rubber toward home plate.

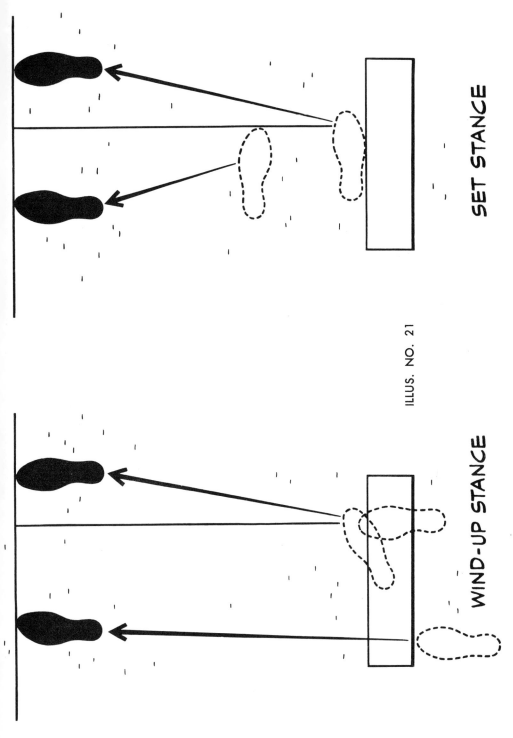

SET STANCE

WIND-UP STANCE

ILLUS. NO. 21

83

Procedure

Place a pitcher on the rubber and a catcher in his box. With the pitcher's pivot foot on the rubber, draw a straight line from that foot toward home plate. Then have the pitcher throw a ball at normal speed to the catcher. Note that his striding foot, if he is right handed, lands to the left of the line drawn from his pivot foot, but that it is to the right of the line if he is left handed. At the point where his striding foot contacts the ground, draw another line at right angles to the first line. Be sure that his pivot foot, on the follow-through, moves to, but not over, the line which crosses the first line. (Note Illustration No. 21. Observe that these drawings are for right handers, and that the striding would be reversed for left handed pitchers. Note also, pitcher's pivot foot is in front of rubber, not on top of it.)

93. Pitcher Follow-Through Drill

Purpose

To help the pitcher learn to follow through properly, both from the set and the wind-up positions.

Procedure

While on the mound, the pitcher takes his normal delivery as in Drill No. 85 (Pitcher Rhythm Drill), and uses the same stance. However, on the follow-through, he reaches down with his pitching hand and picks up dirt or grass on the outside of his striding foot. The feet remain in the same position as in Drill No. 92 (Pitcher Stride Practice.)

94. Fork Ball Pitcher Drill

Purpose

To teach the pitcher the correct method of gripping the baseball for throwing the fork ball.

Procedure

While the pitcher is idle or on the bench, take a ball and place it in his hand in the position for throwing the fork ball. Force the ball between the forked index and middle fingers. This develops the proper grip and spread of the fingers for throwing the fork ball.

Daily work on this grip and forcing the ball between the fingers will develop a better and more comfortable fork ball grip.

95. Pick-Off Plays

Purpose

To teach the pitcher the proper movements in making a pick-off, thus preventing a called balk, and keeping runners close to the base.

Pitchers should practice their pick-off movements on the side with other players or without a ball.

Procedure

Place the pitcher on the mound, infielders in their positions, and runners on base. The pitcher attempts pick-offs for the following situations. All throws should be knee high at the corner of the bag nearest the runner.

A. *First Base:*
1. *With the first baseman holding the runner on base,* the pitcher throws from all positions—during the stretch, pre-stretch, and when set.
2. *With the first baseman back,* when the pitcher, looking at second through the corner of his eye, sees the first baseman break for the bag, he wheels and throws.

B. *Second Base* (Note Drill No. 42):
1. With the second baseman.
2. With the shortstop.

C. *Third Base* (Note Drill No. 173-A):
1. Stretch positions as for runner on first and third or a possible squeeze play.
2. Wind-up stance.

96. Pitcher Sign Drill

Purpose

To develop the pitchers' and catchers' understanding, and clarification of signs to be used during a game. Shortstop and second baseman must be included in this drill.

Procedure

Have pitchers and infielders line up facing catchers with approximately 60½ feet between them. While they are in a catching stance, have the catchers give the signs which will be used in a game situation. These should include signs for a fast ball, curve, change-of-pace, pick-off, pitch-out, and change of sign. After each sign given by the catcher, the pitcher or infielder should tell the catcher what the sign was, and there should be an agreement on all signs. However, if there is a case where a pitcher with bad eyes cannot see the signs given by the catcher, reverse the procedure and have the pitcher give the signs while the catcher calls out the correct answers.

97. Batting Practice Throwing Schedule

Purpose

To see that all pitchers get enough work and that some pitchers do not get too much work.

Procedure

A daily chart of how many minutes a pitcher worked should be made. It should include the pitcher's name, how long he worked, and on what days. When practice games begin, change the minutes into innings pitched. Work all pitchers equally for about two weeks. Then, after three weeks, separate starters from the others. This is done after pitchers are in fairly good shape.

See that starters get plenty of work; don't let them off with too little work.

98. Alternate Batting Practice Pitcher Drill

Purpose

To get the most possible batting practice out of a small pitching staff.

Procedure

After two pitchers have loosened up, one of them throws 20 pitches to batters, and then the other pitcher throws 20. They pick up balls for each other when not pitching, and they also wear jackets when not pitching. These two pitchers alternate after every twentieth pitch until each has thrown 60 pitches. In the meantime, two other pitchers should have been loosening up for their turns. They repeat the same procedure used by the first two. If there are two more pitchers, they loosen up and relieve the second pair after those two have pitched 60 balls each as described above.

Pitchers throw at half to three-quarter speed. After completing the first week of practice, each can change from 20 pitches to 10 minutes of pitching for a turn. Then, after pitchers are in good shape, they can take turns of 15 to 20 minutes each.

99. Rotation of Pitchers

Purpose

To keep a daily rotation on all pitchers so that they obtain an equal amount of work.

Procedure

When No. 1 pitcher, who will start batting practice, is warmed up sufficiently, he starts pitching to the batters. When he has about five minutes left to throw, No. 2 pitcher starts warming up on the side lines. While No. 1 pitcher is throwing, No. 3 pitcher is picking up balls for No. 1, and No. 4 is shagging balls into the outfield or is engaged in some other drill.

When No. 1 has completed this pitching, he immediately goes into another drill before he cools off. Then No. 2 goes in to pitch; No. 3 goes to the side lines to warm up, and No. 4 picks up balls for No. 2.

This rotation keeps going until all pitchers have pitched their share of batting practice.

During the first week of practice, pitcher rotation should be about every 5 to 10 minutes, depending on the control and condition of the pitcher. Once they are in shape, they can throw from 10 to 20 minutes if they feel like throwing.

Keep a daily chart of how much and how long each pitcher throws, and make sure all of them get a sufficient amount of batting practice pitching.

100. Game Poise Drill for Pitchers

Purpose

To get the pitchers ready for opponents' jockeying and harassment and to prevent possible balks.

Procedure

Put a pitcher on the rubber, and on command have him step off the rubber. Commands such as, "Time!" or "There he goes!" should be given.

1. In a set stance, not looking at the coach, the pitcher's pivot foot backs off the rubber at the coach's command. Then put runners on bases and have them run when the pitcher is not looking at them. In all cases, the pivot foot must come off the rubber before the ball is taken out of the glove.
2. During some intra-squad games, have base runners harass the pitcher by yelling at him and giving many fake starts from the bases.

   (Note: With the exception of the fake starts, this is not recommended for regular games, since it is unsportsmanlike.)

CHAPTER 7

CATCHING DRILLS

A pitching staff is only as good as its catcher. If a team has a good catcher, it will be a good team. He is the coach on the field and must run the team. His hustle and play can affect the whole team. The following drills are designed to develop the catcher so that he knows what to do, how to do it, and where to go during every play situation.

101. Check-List for Proper Execution

(Note Screening Candidates Drill No. 207.)

102. Catching Body Positions

Purpose

To get the catcher to feel comfortable and at ease in different positions and to look the part of a catcher.

Procedure

Place the catcher behind the plate in full gear. The coach works with him in assuming correct positions and gives him advice when needed.

A. *Giving Signals.* The feet are spread shoulder width with toes pointed straight ahead or slightly toed in, and are parallel. Knees are pointed straight ahead, and the back is leaning slightly forward. The catcher's right elbow is held near the body, and the glove hand is extended off the left knee with the palm facing first base, thumb upward, pointing toward the pitcher. In this position, the catcher gives signals with right hand fitted firmly up against and in his crotch. He may use fingers or hand positions.

B. *Catching Stance with Nobody on Base.* The catcher's feet are spread slightly more than described above. His right toe is parallel to his left heel. His tail is down, not up in the air, and the back is leaning slightly forward. The weight is on the toes. His arms are held away from the body and are half extended toward the pitcher. The right foot may be pointed slightly outward. (Note Illustration No. 18.) Although he can catch with the right knee on the ground, the catcher must be ready for the bunt or pop fly. The catcher judges his distance behind the hitter by assuming his crouch and reaching up with his glove toward the batter's back elbow. The glove should miss his elbow by several inches.

C. *Catching Stance with Runners on Base.* With men on base, everything is the same except that the tail is higher, knees are bent less, and the catcher never catches with one knee on the ground.

D. *Giving the Target.* The palm of the glove is facing the pitcher, fingers up, thumb in. The catcher is in a sitting crouch, as described above. In case a low target is needed, the catcher, in order to avoid a low crouch, especially with men in running position, simply turns his glove with fingers pointed down, thumb out, and the palm facing the pitcher.

E. *Position of Bare Hand and Glove.* The right thumb is under the index finger, and the fingers are curled, but not clenched. The hand, which is held against the glove, turns counterclockwise as the ball approaches the glove. Then the back of the hand and fingers are facing the ball, not pointing toward it as it approaches. As the ball hits the glove, the hand covers it.

103. Sign Drills—Pitchers, Catchers, and Infielders

(Note Drill No. 96.)

104. Across-Seam Ball Grip for Catchers

Purpose

To teach catchers to grip a baseball across the seams, at the widest spread of the seams, in order to reduce sliding and sailing of the ball when thrown by the catcher.

Procedure

While playing catch, each time a catcher receives a ball he quickly grips the ball across the seams, removes it from his glove, and makes a snap throw. Without looking at the ball he must be sure of this grip before throwing quickly. (Note Illustration No. 22, page 92.)

105. Footwork Drill—Intentional Walk

Purpose

To help the catcher develop the proper footwork for all plays.

Procedure

A. *Throwing to Bases:*

Set up the drills listed in Drill No. 106. Place the catcher behind the plate and throw balls to him. Before each pitch, yell the play situation and which base or bases runners are on. After catching the pitch, the catcher sets his feet and hand as to throw, but does not actually throw the ball. During the drill, which has a batter at the plate, the coach makes any necessary corrections in the catcher's footwork.

B. *Intentional Walk:*

Purpose

To keep the catcher and the pitcher from balking and to show the pitcher where the ball is to be thrown.

Procedure

Place the pitcher on the mound, the catcher in full gear behind the plate, and a batter in the batter's box.

The pitcher assumes a set stance and must come to a full stop prior to his delivery.

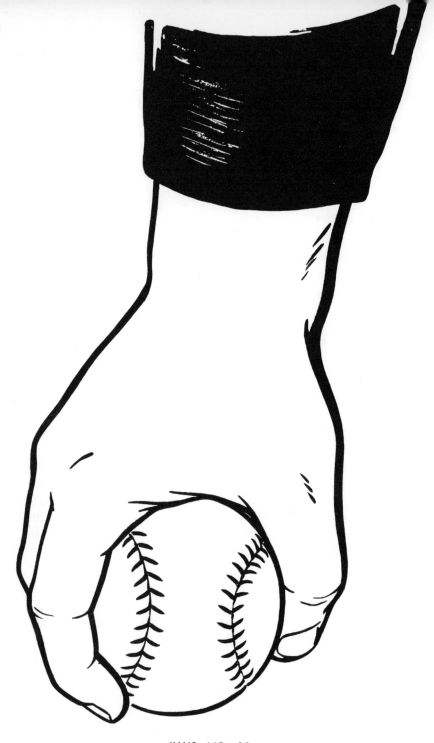

ILLUS. NO. 22

The catcher stays in his area until the ball leaves the pitcher's hand, then moves outside his area away from the batter to receive the ball. The pitcher throws at half speed, missing the plate by two or two and one-half feet, on the side opposite the batter. The batter should try to hit balls that are thrown close to him or across the plate.

Work with both right and left handed hitters. The catcher takes a position in his area on the opposite side of the hitter.

106. Steps for Throwing

Purpose

To teach the catcher the proper steps for throwing to all bases.

Procedure

Have the pitcher throw balls to the catcher to work the following steps:

A. *Throw to First Base.* Usually the throw to first base is a pitch-out on the right side of the catcher.

The right foot steps out toward first base when receiving the ball. The catcher pivots on the right foot, steps with the left, and throws.

Another situation with a left handed hitter is as follows: The right foot, which is about six inches behind the left foot, points toward first base, so that the batter is between the runner and the catcher when the catcher is crouching. When the pitch is caught, the catcher makes the throw to first base with a side-arm flip, very similar to that which the second baseman makes to the shortstop by pivoting his hips instead of his feet. It need not be a pitch-out.

B. *Throw to Second Base.* In this case the catcher does not use a deep knee-bend, but he does keep his tail down, knees bent slightly in a crouch.

If the pitch is to the catcher's right, he steps out with his right foot, plants it, steps with his left foot directly toward second base, and throws.

When the pitch is straight in, the catcher takes a quick crow-hop of only three or four inches toward second, and throws. The hop will be to the right foot and is started when he receives the ball.

If the pitch is to the catcher's left, he strides to the left with his left foot as the ball is being caught, crow-hops to his right foot when the ball is caught, steps toward second base with his left foot, and throws.

C. *Throw to Third Base.* Throws for pick-offs should be two feet on the inside of the bag, and throws on steals should be knee-high on the bag.

    1. *Left handed hitter:*

        (a) If the pitch is down the middle or is to the catcher's left, he makes the catch, crow-hops, and makes a snap throw.

        (b) If the pitch is to his right, the catcher steps out on his right foot and throws.

    2. *Right handed hitter:*

        (a) A pitch made to the right side or down the middle presents very few problems. The catcher simply steps out and toward the pitch with his right foot and throws as he steps toward third with his left.

        (b) On pitches to the left side, into the hitter, the catcher steps toward the ball with his left foot to receive the ball, but leaves the right foot in position. He then hops to his right foot, away from the hitter and toward the pitcher, and steps toward third with his left foot on the throw.

D. *Blocked Ball at Home Plate—Throw to Pitcher Covering.* If the ball is in the dirt near the plate, the catcher picks it up with his bare hand and gives it a firm knee-high toss to the pitcher, who is covering the plate. Pick-up is made by first pressing the ball into the dirt.

E. *Ball at Backstop—Throw to Pitcher Covering.* The catcher approaches the ball as fast as possible, plants his right foot at the right side of the ball, and makes a quick knee-high throw to the pitcher covering the plate. The catcher should attempt to pick up the ball with two hands, but the position of the ball will determine this. The throw can be underhand, side-arm, or overhand, depending upon the time.

F. *Pick-off Play.* (Note Team Drill No. 42.)

107. Ball-in-Dirt Drill

Purpose

To teach catchers to block the ball, then to find it.

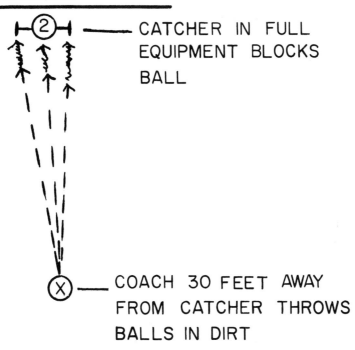

BACKSTOP

CATCHER IN FULL
EQUIPMENT BLOCKS
BALL

COACH 30 FEET AWAY
FROM CATCHER THROWS
BALLS IN DIRT

DRILL NO. 107: Ball in Dirt

Procedure

Put the catcher in full game gear, including a protective cup, against the backstop. Then, from a distance of about 30 feet, throw balls to his left, to his right, and in front of him, making all of them bounce in the dirt. The catcher's job in this drill is not to catch the balls, but to *block them*, and to keep them in front of him.

A. *Balls to the Catcher's Right.* Have the catcher go down on his left knee, chest perpendicular to the path of the ball, with the face of the glove and palm of the hand at a 90-degree angle to the dirt.

B. *Balls to the Catcher's Left.* This is the same routine as above, except that the *right* knee is down.

C. *Balls in Front of the Catcher.* On these balls, the catcher should come down on both knees. It is important that the thumb of his throwing hand be tucked under the index finger with his hand closed. The face of the glove is angled in order to keep the ball in the dirt and so it will not carom off and up over the catcher.

108. Wild Pitch Drill

(Note Drill No. 84.)

109. Arm Strengthener to Develop Correct Throwing Form

Purpose

To develop the catcher's arm and throwing form.

Procedure

The catcher assumes an upright stance with his feet parallel and spread a little wider than his shoulders. When warming up a pitcher and the ball is received, he brings his throwing hand up and straight back beside his ear. Without moving his feet, using a sharp, snappy overhand motion, he throws the ball back to the pitcher. As he gets warmer, he can throw harder, and he can throw the distance from home to second base without moving his feet if some player will receive the ball.

This should be practiced every time the catcher warms up a pitcher or plays catch.

110. Catcher Making Tag Plays at Home

Purpose

To teach the catcher to make the tag properly while preventing injury to himself.

Procedure

Place a temporary soft base in a grassy area. The catcher should be in full equipment, and runners should be instructed to slide into this base. (However, the runners should not use spikes.) The catcher assumes his position in front of the base, as if it were home plate. His left foot is on the middle front of the base, permitting runners to see the back half of it. When the runner can see the back half of the base, he is more likely to go for it and not try to make contact with the catcher to take him out of the play. Timed to barely beat the runner coming into the base, a ball is thrown to the catcher, who attempts to tag the runner. (Note Sliding Drill No. 200.)

Proper procedure for the tag: The catcher drops his knees just in front of the base and makes the tag, which can be made in two ways: (1) The catcher grips the ball in his right hand, with his hand and the ball in the pocket of the mitt. (2) He can grip the ball in his right hand and place it four to six inches behind the pocket of the mitt with the back of the mitt facing the runner. By this method the runner hits the mitt and knocks it into the ball, thus taking the shock off the hand holding the ball.

111. Catcher Making Force-Out Play at Home

Purpose

To teach the catcher the proper procedure in making the force-out play at home plate.

The catcher must remember that the runner is trying to knock him down and break up the play. The catcher takes a position in front of the plate, toward the play, with his right foot on the plate. As soon as he receives the ball, he crow-hops off the base and makes his throw.

If the catcher does not have time to get off the base, he takes the ball on the move, steps on the base with his right foot, crow-hops off to throw or throws directly off the plate.

Procedure

Have all infielders throw from their positions to the catcher, who receives the ball, tags the plate as above, and throws to first, second, or third base, for an additional out. This can be performed in regular team infield practice drills.

112. Double Steal Prevention

Purpose

To help the catcher develop skill in holding a runner on third while attempting to throw out a runner going to second base.

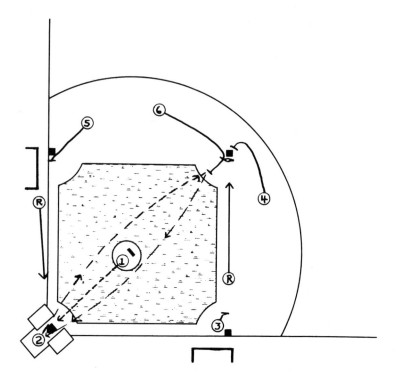

DRILL NO. 112: Double Steal Prevention

Procedure

With runners on first and third bases, when an attempted double steal is made, the catcher quickly fakes to third with his head and shoulders, causing the runner to return to third, then throws to second base.

In every infield practice, before the catcher throws to second base, make him look at third base. This should be repeated until it becomes a habit. (Note Second Base Drill No. 142-B.)

113. Fielding Bunts

Purpose

To teach the catcher the proper way to field bunts to throw to the bases.

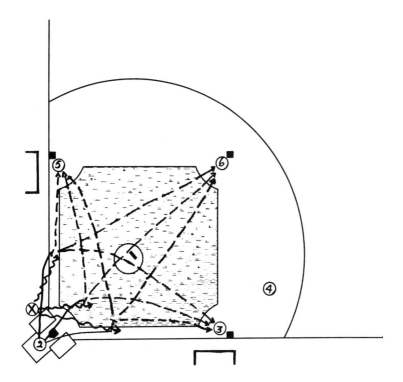

DRILL NO. 113: Fielding Bunts

Procedure

Put the defensive infield in position and runners on bases where needed. The coach rolls balls in front of the plate, and the pitcher lets the catcher make the plays.

A. *First Base Area:*

   1. Throw to First Base:

      The catcher breaks out on the bunt, fields the ball with both hands as the palm of the glove hand faces the ball and properly stops the roll of the ball. He takes a crow-hop, waltz step, or side step, bringing his right foot behind his left toward the middle of the infield, and throws three-quarters or overhand to first base. Caution should be taken not to throw directly down the base line. Avoid hitting the runner or making the first baseman field the ball into the runner.

2. Throw to Second Base:

The catcher fields the ball as above, crow-hops, and throws overhand to second base.

3. Throw to Third Base:

The catcher works himself into a good throwing position before fielding the ball. He fields the ball as above, and then throws side-arm or underhand if he needs to in order to save time.

B. *Third Base Area:*

1. Throw to First Base:

The catcher works himself to the left of the ball before fielding it with both hands, spins clockwise, and throws three-quarters or underhand to first base.

2. Throw to Second Base:

The catcher charges the ball, positions himself to the left of the ball, fields it, crow-hops, and throws overhand to second.

3. Throw to Third Base:

In this situation the catcher charges straight at the ball, fields it as above, and if possible throws overhand chest high to third.

Alternate Drill No. 82 with the pitcher. When the pitcher fields the ball, the catcher should call the play. He should tell the pitcher the base to which he should throw.

114. Pop Fly Practice

Purpose

To give catchers needed practice in handling pop flies, which are always tough to handle in full gear, behind the batter.

Procedure

With the catcher in full gear, the coach or another player hits pop flies for the catcher to field. This should be done for fifteen minutes two to three times weekly. Also note Team Drill No. 37 for extra practice.

115. Catcher Covering First and Third Bases

Purpose

To teach the catcher how, when, and where to cover these bags properly.

Procedure

A. *Backing Up Throw to First Base.* Hit the ball to an infielder, and have a runner at the plate break for first base. The catcher breaks for a position near the fence or dugout, backing up the throw where an overthrown ball would go.

B. *With a Runner on First Base.* The catcher breaks for the above positions if the play or out is completed at second base. If the runner is not out at second, the catcher continues for the back-up of first base. If the ball is caught at first, he breaks back for home. If it is an overthrow, the pitcher must cover home, since the catcher will pick up the overthrow.

C. *Making a Pick-Off Play at First Base on Short Hit to Right Field. Nobody on Base.* Hit a ball in the hole between first and second basemen. Both of them make an attempt to field the ball. As the hitter, noting the first baseman not on the bag, makes his turn toward second, the catcher, who followed the runner, covers first base for the throw from right field, and the pitcher backs up the catcher. (Note Drill No. 185-A.)

D. *Covering Third Base on a Bunt.* Put infielders in their respective positions and a runner on first base only. Bunt a ball to the third baseman. The catcher covers third base. The runner on first breaks with the pitch and continues to third on the bunt. The first baseman attemps to throw the runner out at third with the catcher taking the throw.

CHAPTER 8

GENERAL

INFIELD DRILLS

Basically, there are certain fundamentals that all infielders must know and have the skill to execute. An infielder must know where he is on the field and be able to throw a ball to a base with his eyes closed. He must know what his team members can do and will do, and he must help them when the need exists. The following drills are designed to improve the skills of the infielder, and, more specifically, to have him at the right place, at the right time, in condition mentally and physically, ready to play every day.

116. Proper Technique for Fielding Ground Balls

Purpose

To improve fielding, give players more confidence, and help make them look the part of ball players.

Procedure

Put a fielder in his position and hit balls to him until he meets the following check points:

A. *Right-Hander* (Illustration No. 23, see page 116):
  1. Left foot in front of his right foot. Left heel lines up almost parallel with his right foot.
  2. Feet spread slightly wider than shoulder width.

3. Tail down.
4. Head up.
5. Knees bent.
6. Glove carried low, barely touching the ground, and out in front of the body.
7. Keep eyes on the ball.
8. When the ball hits the glove, let the hands move in *toward* the body, but not *against* the body. Give with the force of the ball.
9. Crow-hop and throw.
B. *Left-Hander:*
   Same as above (for right-hander), except that the opposite foot will be forward.

117. Touch Grass Right and Left

Purpose

To help all players to move properly to their right and left while running in a low crouch, and to serve as a good conditioner.

Procedure

1. Line up pitchers, infielders, outfielders, and catchers with gloves on in the outfield area. Have players in columns, five to six feet apart, four or five to the column, with the columns 10 to 12 feet apart, players facing the coach.
2. Coach gets players in fielding position by commanding "Hands on knees."
3. On command, "Break left," or "Break right," each player uses the cross-over step and moves 10 to 12 steps in that direction while touching his glove to the grass with each step. Team stops, gets set and returns to its original position when coach commands, "Break."
4. Repeat until team looks tired.
5. Give a short break.
6. Give Conditioning Drill No. 13 (Deep Breathing, Squat, and Leg Shake) until team looks ready to go.
7. Another short break.

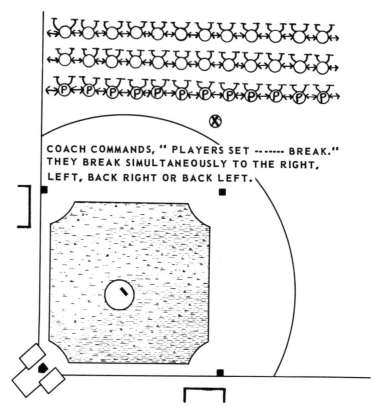

COACH COMMANDS, " PLAYERS SET ------- BREAK."
THEY BREAK SIMULTANEOUSLY TO THE RIGHT,
LEFT, BACK RIGHT OR BACK LEFT.

DRILL NO. 117: Touch Grass Right and Left

8. Command, "Hands on knees. Ready for breaking back on fly balls."
9. Now command, "Break back to left," or "Break back to right." Players break, but do not touch ground with glove.
10. Players walk back to starting position.
11. Repeat until the team looks tired.

118. Orientation Drill

Purpose

To help infielders learn where bases are located to the point that they can throw accurately without first looking for the base.

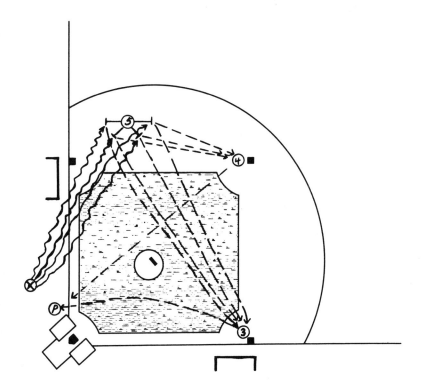

DRILL NO. 118: Orientation

Procedure

Put an infielder in his position and a first baseman at first so that the infielder can throw to him. Have another player or the coach take five to eight balls and hit them rapid fire to the infielder. As soon as he has fielded, thrown to first, and before he is quite set, the hitter should hit another ball.

After the fielder has thrown 15-20 balls to first base, place a fielder at second base, and repeat the process, except that the throw goes to second base. Continue until the infielder is tired, and then replace him with another fielder until each is well oriented as to where bases are located.

119. Equilibrium Drill

Purpose

To teach players how to judge a fly ball after they have misjudged it. Also, how to keep their balance to make the proper play.

Procedure

A. *Misjudged Fly Balls.* With infielders in position, the coach hits high fly balls to them, one at a time. When the ball has reached its greatest height, the infielder, for whom it was hit, turns completely around once before making the catch. After he is acquainted with the drill, he may turn around two or three times. Each infielder takes his turn.

B. *(Note Gimmick No. 239—Rolla-Rolla Board).* Fly ball practice should be given on three different type days. One day should have a clear sunny sky, one day a cloudy sky and one should be a windy day.

120. Run-Down Play Drill

Purpose

To teach infielders the proper procedure for making the run-down play with the minimum number of throws. The secret is chasing the base runner going at full speed.

Procedure

Place infielders and outfielders in their normal positions, and place runners on bases. Then pick or catch them off, with the outfielders backing up every play.

A. *Runner Between First and Second.* The pitcher catches the runner off at first. The first baseman then runs him toward second base where the shortstop or second baseman is standing three feet in front of second with the other player backing him up at the bag. While the left and centerfielders move in to back up the play at second, the right fielder comes in to cover first base, and the catcher, if there are no other runners on base, moves down the line to back him up.

When the runner is approximately 15 feet from the infielder stand-

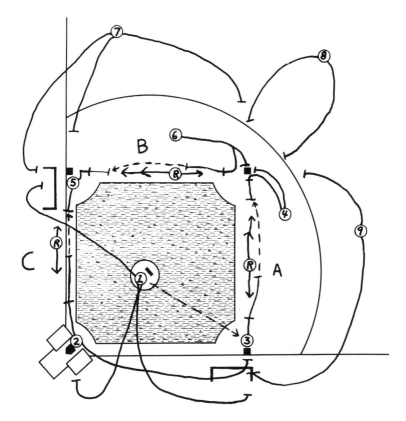

DRILL NO. 120: Run-Down Play

ing in front of second, the fielder breaks toward the runner; first baseman throws the ball to him, and the fielder makes the tag.

B. *Runner Between Second and Third.* Have the runner caught
off second base. The shortstop or second baseman chases him toward
third base at full speed. The play is made in the same manner as that
in "A" above. With all fielders backing up the play, the third baseman breaks for the runner, receives the ball from the player chasing
the runner, and makes the tag.

C. *Runner Between Third and Home.* Hit a ball to the third baseman. When it is hit, the runner breaks for home and attempts to
score on the play. The ball is fielded and thrown to the catcher, who

chases the runner back toward third at full speed. He then throws to the third baseman, who is three feet in front of the bag. The same procedure is followed as in the first base drill. The shortstop covers third base, behind the third baseman.

D. *Ball Hit to the Pitcher.* Have a runner on any base, and let him break for the next base. The job of the pitcher when he fields a ball in this case is to determine where the runner is going. If the runner sees that he is caught and hesitates, the pitcher should run directly at him to make the runner commit himself. When he does this, the pitcher throws to the fielder covering the base which the runner tries to take. However, if the runner is three-fourths of the way to the next base and does not hesitate, the pitcher throws to the base ahead of him. If he is only one-fourth of the distance to the next base, the throw should be to the base behind him. Then, the run-down starts when the ball is received from the pitcher, and it is completed as in the above drills.

121. Multiple Infield Practice

Purpose

To give infielders maximum ground ball practice.

Procedure

Put all infielders, including extras, in position. Each fielding position has a fungo hitter who hits to that position only.

> A. The fungo hitter hits a ball to the fielder in his position. If there are extra fielders, they take turns. Fielders throw the ball directly back to the fungo hitter's pick-up man.
>
> B.
>
> 1. Put a second baseman on second. The player or players at third now throw to second base, and the ball is returned to their fungo hitter. Extra second basemen continue to field balls hit to them, but they take turns receiving balls thrown from the third baseman. (Follow Drill No. 121, diagram.)
>
> 2. Following the above drill, have the third baseman throw

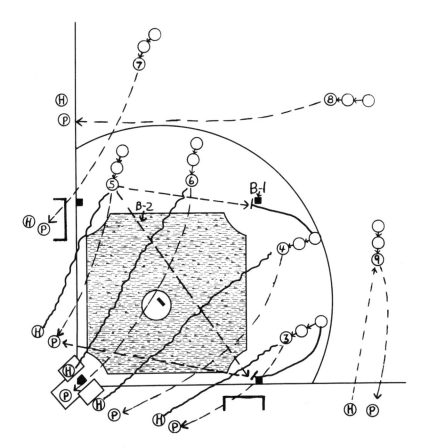

DRILL NO. 121: Multiple Infield—Outfield Practice

to an extra first baseman covering first. The first baseman returns the ball to the fungo hitter. Extra first basemen continue to field balls hit to them but take turns covering the bag for thrown balls. (Follow Drill No. 121, diagram.)

C.
1. The fungo hitter hits a ball to the first baseman, who throws to third.
2. Fungo hitter hits ball to the first baseman, who throws to second base, which is covered by a shortstop, as in Drill B-1 above.

D.

1. The shortstops throw to first base as their fungo hitter hits to them.
2. The shortstops throw to second base, second baseman to first.

E.

1. Second basemen throw to first as their fungo hitter hits to them.
2. Second basemen throw to shortstop at second, who throws to first.

Fungo hitters continue hitting to players in their positions while Drills B to D are worked. Caution must be applied to use only one drill at a time. Fungos must not be hit to a player who is fielding a thrown ball while covering a base.

122. Stuffed Glove (Especially for double play)

(Note Gimmick No. 240.)

123. Duty Drills During Infield Pre-Game Practice

Purpose

To develop a well-organized infield practice, performed as snappily as possible.

Procedure

Place infield players in their respective positions. The coach then hits medium speed ground balls to the infielders, giving them confidence in their fielding. The coach hits to all positions, and the players take a typical infield practice with plenty of "holler and hustle."

The following are check points to note for each infield position:

A. *Catcher:*

1. Equipment can be worn.
2. All throws should be hard, firm, and chest high.
3. He should receive balls behind the plate and throw from there.

4. On all throws to second base, he "looks" the runner back to third before throwing to second.
5. On bunts, the catcher should charge out and place his body in position to throw, as in Drill No. 113.
6. Good hard throwing in practice will discourage game-time stealing.
7. Practice Drill No. 111—Force-Out Play.

B. *First Baseman:*
1. Fields thrown balls and makes certain to tag the base on every play.
2. Throws hard and accurately to the catcher behind the plate.
3. Throws hard to shortstop and third baseman on the bag.
4. Throws should be overhand whenever possible, and they should be chest high.

C. *Second Baseman and Shortstop:*
1. Snappy overhand throws whenever possible.
2. Cover the bases and back up plays when necessary.
3. Practice Alternate Double Play—Drill No. 148.
4. Practice Optional Double Play—Drill No. 159.

D. *Third Baseman:*
1. Snappy overhand throws.
2. Covers the bag and backs up plays when necessary.
3. Fields slow bunts.

Situation Play
When the ball is hit to first base for one out, the first baseman throws to the shortstop covering second, who throws to the third baseman to pick off runner rounding third, as in Drill No. 159.

124. Game Condition Infield Practice

Purpose

To get all infielders acquainted with game condition plays.

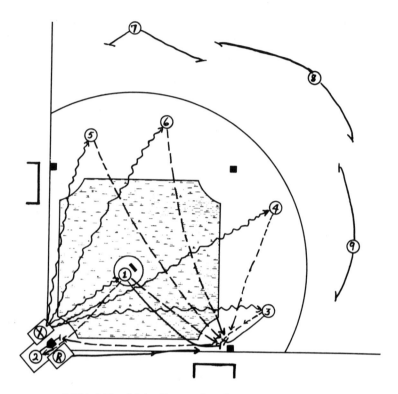

DRILL NO. 124: Game Condition Infield Practice

Procedure

Have the infielders assume their respective positions, with a pitcher on the mound and a catcher behind the plate. Use outfielders and pitchers as base runners.

The pitcher throws a ball to the catcher. The coach, who stands at the plate, hits another ball to the infield—either a ground ball or a line drive. Just as the coach hits the ball, a player standing in the batter's box drops his bat and runs to first base. The infield tries to throw him out. However, if the runner is safe, he stays on base as in a game situation, thus setting up a double play situation.

The coach hits to different positions as the runners run the bases.

A first baseman who knows how to catch the ball and play the bag properly can develop good infielders. If an infielder can throw the ball to first base without worrying about a perfect throw, he will field and throw better. A good first baseman can help the pitcher to keep runners close to the bag, resulting in a force-out at second. Pitchers should be able to throw to first with confidence. The following drills are designed to help a first baseman learn his position well and to develop into a good fielder.

CHAPTER 9

FIRST BASEMAN

DRILLS

125. Check-List for Proper Execution

(Note Screening Candidates Drill No. 207.)

126. In-Place Reach and Field Drill

Purpose

To give players an idea of how far they can reach and still field the ball while keeping their feet in place or by taking one cross-over step.

In addition to the purpose mentioned above, this drill also helps infielders and pitchers develop the quick reflex action so necessary for handling the hard smashes they are faced with during game situations. Gimmick No. 239 will aid the player for this situation.

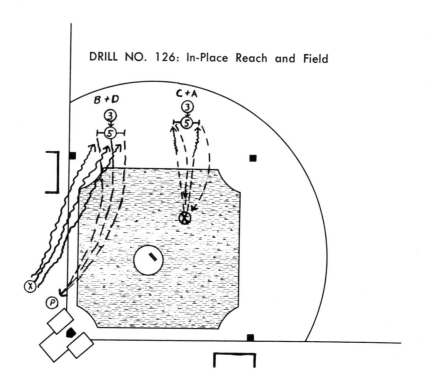

DRILL NO. 126: In-Place Reach and Field

Procedure

Put infielders in fielding positions, feet spread comfortably about shoulder width apart. Fielders should be crouched, knees slightly bent, weight distributed evenly on the balls of the feet, parallel and slightly toed-in or pointed straight ahead. Their arms should hang loosely out from and in front of the body, so that the glove and throwing hand are carried low. (Note Illustration No. 23, page 116.)

After the fielders are in position, the coach should stand about 20 feet away with a supply of baseballs.

A. *Fielding Thrown Balls.* The coach throws line drives, one-hoppers, and ground balls to the left and right of the fielders. The fielders must field the balls by reaching and keeping their feet in place.

B. *Fielding Batted Balls.* From 90 feet the coach hits the same type of balls he threw from 20 feet, and fielders must field them by reaching only, no stepping.

C. *Fielding Thrown Balls with a Cross-Over Step.* The same procedure is followed as in "A," except fielders are permitted to take one cross-over step, since the coach throws the balls farther to the right and left.

D. *Fielding Batted Balls with a Cross-Over Step.* This is the same as "B," except that a cross-over step is permitted, since the coach hits balls farther to the right and left.

127. Break for and Cover First Base

Purpose

To teach the first baseman how to find first base and to get to the bag quickly after the ball has been hit.

Procedure

Place a first baseman in his fielding position and have balls hit to another infielder. When the ball is hit, the first baseman breaks for the bag. When he is about four feet from the bag he turns clockwise and hops to the bag, facing the fielder who is throwing the ball. The first baseman's heels touch the corners of the bag. (Note Drill Nos. 128 and 129.)

To keep the first baseman from breaking for first too quickly, hit some balls near his fielding position. This will keep him "honest"—in that he will not leave his position until he sees whether the ball is hit into his fielding area.

128. Shifting of Feet When Tagging the Base

Purpose

To give the first baseman better balance in the fielding position on thrown balls.

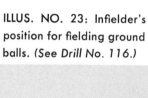

ILLUS. NO. 23: Infielder's position for fielding ground balls. (See *Drill No. 116.*)

ILLUS. NO. 24: Correct position for the First Baseman in receiving thrown balls. (See *Drill No. 128.*)

Procedure

Place the first baseman at the bag, and throw balls to his left and right, high and low. On balls directly at a right handed first baseman, his right foot tags the bag, and his left foot goes out toward the throw. It is reversed for the left handed first baseman.

A. *The Well-Coordinated First Baseman.* The well-coordinated player should shift his feet on balls thrown to one side or the other. On balls to his right, his left foot tags the bag, and on balls to his left, his right foot tags the bag.

B. *The Uncoordinated First Baseman.* This player need not shift his feet. However, if he is right handed, his right foot touches the base on all throws. And if he is left handed, his left foot always tags the bag.

Note: Prior to the throw, the first baseman breaks toward the base. His heels touch the inner corners of the bag. He strides to meet the ball. His striding foot hits the dirt just as the ball hits his glove. This keeps his other foot on the bag.

The foot tagging the bag should be turned sideways, with the inside of the foot facing the dirt and the toe of the foot tagging the bag. The first baseman never kicks the bag or at the bag on the catch, unless the throw pulls him off, but goes from the bag on the catch. (Note Illustration No. 24, page 116.)

129. Fielding Throws

Purpose

To teach the first baseman to get into position to field all throws.

Procedure

Have all infielders in their respective positions. The coach hits balls to all infield positions, and the first baseman breaks for the bag to take the throw.

A. *Second Base, Third Base, Shortstop:*

In fielding balls thrown from the above three positions, the first baseman tries to face the fielder throwing the ball.

B. *Catcher:*

1. On slow hits or bunts, the first baseman places his left

foot on the bag and his right foot in the infield, giving the catcher a good target inside the base line.

2. On a ball that is in foul territory on the first base side— such as a pass ball or missed third strike—the first baseman puts his right foot on the bag and his left foot in foul territory, receiving the ball outside the base line.

C. *First Baseman as Relay Man:*

The first baseman will take throws from right field on balls hit into deep right field foul territory. This is the only play in which a first baseman normally would go out as a relay man.

D. *The First Baseman as Cut-Off Man:*

The first baseman acts as cut-off man on all throws to home plate from right and center fields. On throws from right field, he lines up the throw and is in the grass area between the mound and first base. On throws from center field, he gets behind the mound, lining up the throw so the throw will not hit the mound.

130. Pitcher Teamwork Drill

Purpose

To teach the pitcher the proper way to approach and cover first base, and to teach the first baseman the proper way to give him the ball.

Procedure

Put a pitcher on the mound and a first baseman in position for the following plays. The coach rolls or hits the ball to the first baseman, who throws to the pitcher covering first base.

A. *Deep Throw.* The ball is hit to the first baseman's right, near the second baseman's position. The first baseman fields the ball and throws it to the pitcher approximately three feet before he hits the bag. The throw should be overhand and at medium speed.

B. *Close Throw.* The coach hits the ball to the first baseman near the bag, who tosses it to the pitcher, chest high, before he hits the bag. The throw is an underhand toss, with the palm of the hand facing the pitcher. When the first baseman tosses, he moves with the ball, stepping toward the pitcher in a follow-through. The ball must not hang in the air, but the toss must be *firm*.

C. *Fielding Bunt*. The coach rolls the ball between the pitcher and the first baseman. If the pitcher sees that he can field the ball, he yells, "I got it!" and the first baseman gets out of the way, moving toward first. Normally, the second baseman covers first on this play. If the pitcher cannot get it, he yells, "Take it!" and breaks for the bag, allowing the first baseman to field the ball.

131. Holding the Runner on Base

Purpose

To help the first baseman learn how to hold the runner on the base, then break from the bag on the pitch to be in position to field the ball if it is hit to his area.

The fundamentals involved in the drill are as follows: The first baseman takes a position with his left foot on or near the foul line. The right foot is on the inside corner of the base nearest the pitcher. The glove is held just off the right knee as a target for the pitcher. The tag is made in a sweeping motion back to the base. Let the runner come to the base rather than going to him. When no pick-off is attempted and the pitch is being made, the first baseman takes two quick steps toward second base and gets set to field the batted ball. An exception would be on a possible bunt. Then he must break toward home.

Procedure

The pitcher holds the runner on the base, sometimes attempting to pick him off and sometimes pitching to the catcher. On the pitch, the first baseman takes two quick steps to get into fielding position. As the pitcher throws, the coach hits to the first baseman, who fields the ball and throws it to the pitcher to continue the drill. Add a bunt situation.

132. Teamwork with the Second Baseman

(Note Second Base Drill No. 140.)

133. Fielding Bunts and Throwing Drill

Purpose

To teach first basemen how to get into position to throw, and throw accurately at the bases when fielding a bunt.

Procedure

Place infielders in respective positions. The coach throws or rolls balls to the first baseman, who throws to one of the following bases:

A. *Third Base.* Left or right handed first baseman charges the ball, fields it on the run if possible, rounds off to get into position, and throws chest high to the third baseman for a force-out, knee high for a tag-out. Use a crow-hop throw if an emergency throw is not necessary.

B. *Second Base.* The first baseman charges the ball, fielding it on the run if possible. The left handed first baseman pivots clockwise and throws overhand if possible, using a crow-hop if an emergency throw is not necessary.

The right handed first baseman fields the ball with his back toward second base, pivots counterclockwise, uses a crow-hop if possible, and throws overhand to second base if possible.

C. *First Base.* The left-hander charges the ball, fields it, pivots clockwise, and throws to first base. The right-hander does the same, but pivots counterclockwise.

D. *Home Plate.* Both right- and left-handers charge ball, field it, and throw overhand or underhand, whichever is needed. The throw must be a firm, hard toss, chest high for a force-out, knee high for a tag-out.

134. Taking Throws from the Catcher on Pick-Off Plays

Purpose

To teach the first baseman to break for the bag, catch the ball, and tag the base runner. It may be necessary to take throws on the run.

Procedure

Have a pitcher on the mound, catcher behind the plate, a runner on first base, and a first baseman in his position. Use pitch-out for this drill.

A. *Bunt Situation.* Start the play with a prearranged sign between the first baseman and the catcher. The first baseman holds the runner on base before the pitch is made. The runner takes an exceptional lead and the first baseman moves toward home taking only about five steps on the pitch. The first baseman returns quickly toward the bag and receives the throw from the catcher.

B. *Runners on First and Second.* With runners on first and second, the first baseman is back behind the runner in his fielding position, and the runner at first is taking a big lead.

The pitcher delivers the ball to the catcher. When it is 10 to 12 feet in front of the catcher, the first baseman breaks for and straddles the base with his left foot in foul territory near the front corner and the right foot touching the opposite corner, and receives the throw from the catcher.

135. Trailer Play Drill

Purpose

To give shortstop and second baseman practice in attempting a pick-off at second or holding the runner close to second base on extra base hits.

Procedure

Put a team in its defensive position with a hitter at the plate. The coach, who is standing between third and home, hits an extra base hit to left or center field. At the crack of the bat, the hitter runs as though he had hit the ball.

As the runner is on his way to first, the first baseman drifts toward first base. When the runner goes on to second, the first baseman trails him at a distance of 10 to 15 feet, and covers second when the runner breaks for third.

When the ball is hit to left-center field, the left and center fielders give chase; the shortstop drifts out to become the relay man, and the second baseman goes out to back him up, thus leaving second base open. (Note Trailer Play No. 151.)

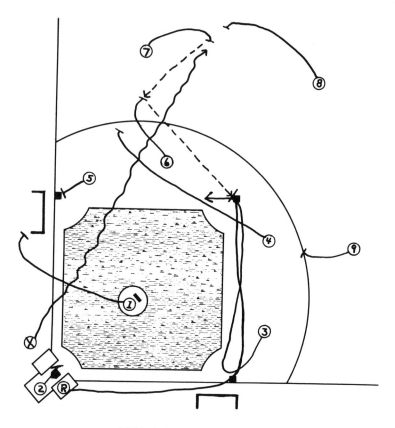

DRILL NO. 135: Trailer Play

136. Pop Fly Drill

(Note Team Drill No. 37.)

Second base is a difficult position to play, and it takes practice and hard work to master it. The second baseman must have no fear of the sliding runner. To overcome fear, he must have confidence in his pivote steps. The following drills are designed to develop a confident, intelligent, well-conditioned second baseman. Teamwork with the shortstop is a key to success. There is no play like the double play to kill an opponent's rally. Work on it daily.

CHAPTER 10

SECOND BASEMAN DRILLS

137. Check-List for Proper Execution

(Note Screening Candidates Drill No. 207.)

138. Fielding and Throwing

Purpose

To help the second baseman learn to get into position for fielding balls and to make the proper throws to bases.

Procedure

The coach hits balls to the second baseman and sets up the following plays.

A. *To First Base:*
   1. The ball is hit to the second baseman's left. If he fields the ball while facing the infield or first base, he

pivots clockwise on his right foot and makes a medium speed throw to the first baseman or pitcher covering first base.

2. The ball is hit to the second baseman's left side, to the deep field position, on the outfield grass toward the right field foul line. He catches the ball, pivots counterclockwise in a complete circle, and makes the throw to first base.

3. The ball is hit directly at the second baseman. He charges the ball in a normal way and throws overhand to first base, either flat-footed or with a crow-hop.

4. The ball is hit to the second baseman's right. He fields the ball and pivots or slides to his right foot, plants the right foot, and throws flat-footed to first. He may sometimes jump into the air and throw while at the top of his jump.

5. The ball is hit over second base—no runner on first base. This drill should be worked during regular infield practice. If the second baseman fields the ball and cannot throw the runner out, he should toss the ball to the shortstop, who throws to first base. This is very similar to a double play.

B. *To Third Base:*

With a runner on second base, the coach hits a line drive or hard ground ball to the second baseman. The runner on second breaks at the crack of the bat. The second baseman fields the ball and:

1. if it is a line drive fly ball, the second baseman makes his throw to second base, where the shortstop is covering;

2. if it is a hard ground ball, he throws to third base to cut off the runner. He should use a crow-hop to the right foot and an overhand throw to the knees of the third baseman.

C. *To Home Plate:*

With the runner on third, the coach hits hard ground balls and slow ground balls to the second baseman. The second baseman takes a position in near the infield grass and fields the ball as he moves toward home. When he fields the ball, he makes an overhand throw to the catcher's knees, having him tag the runner out. On a slowly hit ball he may have to throw underhand or side-armed.

D. *Relays:*

The coach hits balls into the right field and center field for extra base hits, as in Drill Nos. 39 and 40. The second baseman goes out into the relay position for all plays, which means he sets up in a direct line between the outfielder and the base to which the outfielder throws. The outfielder should make the short throw head high and to the glove side of the second baseman. The second baseman should be moving toward the base to which he wants to make the long throw.

139. Fielding Slowly Hit Balls

Purpose

To teach the second baseman how to handle slowly hit balls on the run and to make accurate throws.

Procedure

A. The coach hits slowly bouncing balls to the second baseman in a deep position. He charges the ball, picks it up, and throws underhand to the first baseman.

B. With the second baseman in a position near the infield grass, the coach hits slow balls or push bunts. The fielder fields the ball and throws to first.

Daily work is needed on these drills.

140. Teamwork with the First Baseman

Purpose

To be sure that first base is covered and to prevent unnecessary base hits between the first baseman and the second baseman.

Procedure

Use a pitcher, first baseman, second baseman, and catcher, with the coach as a hitter. The pitcher throws to the catcher, and the coach hits a different infield ball each time.

Ground Ball Between First and Second Base. When the ball is hit, the pitcher breaks for first base as described in Drill No. 83. Both the first baseman and the second baseman break for the ball. Knowing that the pitcher is covering first base, the first baseman takes all he can get. The second baseman runs the play by letting the first baseman take the ball or yelling, "I got it." If the first baseman fields the ball, he pivots and throws to the pitcher covering first. If the second baseman takes the ball, he throws from a clockwise or counterclockwise pivot, depending upon where he fields the ball, as in Drill No. 138-A-1.

141. Fielding Bunts

Purpose

To teach the second baseman to break for first base and receive the throw on a fielded bunt.

Procedure

Use a first baseman, second baseman, third baseman, pitcher, and a catcher. The coach bunts balls or tosses them into proper bunting areas.

A. *Covering First Base.* Since it is a bunting situation, prior to the ball being bunted, the second baseman anticipates the bunt and takes a position closer to the infield and slightly toward first base from his normal playing position. When the ball is bunted, he breaks directly for first base as quickly as possible. He straddles the bag and faces the person fielding and throwing the ball.

B. *Receiving Throws.* Upon straddling the bag, the second baseman faces the player who is throwing the ball and receives it in the same manner as the first baseman in Drill Nos. 128-129. Also note Drill No. 130-C.

142. Receiving Throws

Purpose

To teach the second baseman to get into proper position for throws to second base.

Procedure

A. *Throw from the Pitcher on Batted Balls:*

Place the shortstop and second baseman in position. The coach hits the ball to the pitcher with the second baseman covering second base for the force-out or double play. Prior to the ball's being hit to the pitcher, the second baseman and/or shortstop relays a sign to the pitcher telling him who is covering second base. The shortstop and the second baseman should alternate taking the throw. They back each other up on this play.

B. *Throw from the Catcher on Steals:*

1. On a steal of second base, cover as in Drill No. 143-D.
2. Place runners on first and third and attempt the double steal. The second baseman breaks to a position three or four feet in front of second base, toward the mound. As he is breaking into position, just before he receives the ball, or just after he receives the ball, he looks for the runner on third base to break for home. The shortstop will also aid in calling the play by yelling, "Home," or "Second base." If the play is at home, the second baseman moves in toward home, takes the ball on the run, and throws the ball to the catcher knee high. If the play is at second base, the second baseman stays in position, receives the ball, falls toward the bag to make the tag, and immediately comes up ready to throw home if the runner on third breaks for home.

C. *For other throws see Drill Nos. 143 and 146.*

143. Covering Second Base

Purpose

To teach the second baseman how to handle tag plays and always to see that the bag is covered.

Procedure

A. During Drill No. 37, Pop Fly Drill, insist that the shortstop and the second baseman determine which one will cover second while the other is fielding a ball.

B. When a base on balls is given in a game, be sure that the shortstop or second baseman covers base to prevent the base-on-balls runner from advancing to second base.

C. When receiving throws from the outfield, the second baseman straddles the bag, facing the throw. He places his glove with the ball in it at the edge of the base facing the runner.

D. In taking throws from the catcher, the second baseman again straddles the bag, looking at the throw, receives the ball, and places it on the edge of the base facing the runner.

E. Taking the throw while straddling the bag, the second baseman places the ball in the web of his glove, and places the glove with the ball in it on the edge of the base facing the runner with the back of his index finger, thumb, and web toward the runner. He lets the runner slide into his glove. As soon as the runner hits his glove, he pulls the glove and ball from the play to avoid letting the runner kick the ball out of the glove.

144. On-Base-Line-Tag Double Play

Purpose

To learn how to avoid being run down by the base runner in the base line.

Procedure

Hit slow balls to the second baseman, having him field them in the base line. Do this first without a runner, then with a runner. When the ball has been fielded, the second baseman fakes a backhand throw to second base with his arm, hand, body, and head. In doing this he does not pivot toward second, but steps with his right foot and fakes a backhand toss to second base. He then turns toward the runner, tags him, and throws to first. The fake takes the runner's mind off the act of running the second baseman down. He will then become concerned with the shortstop. (Note Drill No. 145-B for action in faking throw.)

145. Second Baseman as a Starter on the Double Play

To give the second baseman the knowledge, timing, and balance needed in the process of giving the shortstop the ball in the most accurate and best way on the double play.

Procedure

Hit some balls hard and some slowly to the second baseman in the following positions:

A. *Balls Hit Directly at the Second Baseman.* The second baseman should field the ball with his right foot slightly behind his left, legs spread, and both feet planted. He pivots his hips and throws overhand or three-quarters side-arm to the shortstop. There is no pivot of the feet.

B. *Balls Hit to His Right, Near Second Base.* In this situation the second baseman fields balls nearly as above, except that his body may be facing more toward second base. The ball is tossed with a backhand, side-arm motion directly from the glove. The palm of the hand is facing the ground and rotates counterclockwise as the ball is thrown to the shortstop.

C. *Balls Hit to the Second Baseman's Left.* The second baseman gets in front of the ball, catches it, and pivots in a snappy jump motion. His right foot pivots back behind his left, and his left foot pivots toward second base. The ball is thrown either side-arm or three-quarter from this position.

D. *Balls to the Second Baseman's Deep Left.* On these balls the second baseman cannot get in front of them to make the pivot as described in "C" above. Often it is easier to pivot forward, counterclockwise, crossing the right foot in front of the left, planting it out toward the right field foul line, then throwing the ball as the left foot steps toward second. Sometimes a second baseman can make this throw easier by pivoting on his left foot counterclockwise, jumping into the air, and throwing in the jump and pivot.

146. Double Play Drills with Second Baseman as the Middleman

Purpose

To teach the second baseman all possible ways to receive a throw and make the pivots to complete a double play. (Note Detour Drill No. 147, page 132.)

Procedure

The coach hits ground balls to the shortstop, who throws to the second baseman covering second base. The second baseman receives the ball and makes the pivots necessary to complete the double play by throwing to first base. The following are the recommended pivots:

A. *Method 1.* The second baseman moves toward second base, getting there as early as possible, steps on the bag with his right foot, and throws from there. As the left foot hits the dirt on the stride toward first base, the right foot comes up and over the sliding runner, with a slight jump off the left foot. This seems to be the most popular method and the quickest.

Method 2. The second baseman steps on the bag with his right foot, crow-hops from six inches to one foot off the bag on the right foot, and throws from that position.

Method 3. The toughest play is for the second baseman to take the throw on the dead run, tag the bag, pivot and throw. This may occur on some hitters. A good procedure here is for the second baseman to step next to the bag on the side of his approach with his left foot, dragging it across the bag for the tag, then stepping with his right foot, and planting the right foot for an overhand throw. (Note *Method 4* for taking throw on run.)

Method 4. Here is the only pivot where the throw will originate from the left foot. The second baseman may have to take the throw a few steps before he hits the bag. The fastest and best way to make this play is for the left foot to hit the bag, with the second baseman throwing as he comes across the bag, leaping and throwing at the same time to get accuracy and something on the ball.

Method 5. The second baseman tags the bag with his left foot, backs up, and throws when his weight has been shifted to his right foot. Note that tag of the bag is complete before ball is received.

Method 6. The second baseman steps on the bag with his left foot, steps and plants his right foot toward the mound, and throws from there.

Method 7. The second baseman straddles the bag and uses a shift similar to that of a first baseman. When the ball is to his left, his right foot tags the bag, and he throws. With the ball to his right, he tags the bag with his left foot, shifts his weight to his right foot, and throws.

B. *Receiving Throws from the Pitcher.* The coach hits the ball to the pitcher, who fields it, turns, and throws to the second baseman covering second. The second baseman attempts to straddle the bag so that he can shift to either side for the throw. Then he makes one of the above pivots to complete the double play.

C. *Receiving Throws from the Catcher.* When the coach rolls a ball out as though it were bunted, the catcher fields it and throws to the second baseman covering second. The second baseman receives the throw and pivots as above.

D. *Receiving Throws from the Third Baseman.* The coach hits balls to the third baseman in the deep position, close in, to his left, and to his right. The third baseman fields the balls and throws to the second baseman covering second. The second baseman makes a direct approach toward the throw, receives the ball, and makes the pivot steps best suited for completion of the double play.

E. *Receiving Throws from the Shortstop.* The shortstop fields balls hit by the coach and throws to the second baseman covering second. The second baseman gets to the bag as quickly as possible. He approaches the throw in a direct line, but tries to keep his body or shoulders angled slightly toward first base for an easier pivot. He receives the throw and makes the best suited pivot and throw to first base to complete the double play.

F. *Timing the Double Play.* After the double play combination has been thoroughly developed, time the complete action from the hit of the ball until the ball reaches first base. A good double play is made in 3.5 to 4.5 seconds.

147. Detour Drill

Purpose

To teach second basemen efficiency of motion in completing the double play as the middle man.

Procedure

A. Put a second baseman on second base and a first baseman about 10 feet from the second base, directly in line with first and second bases. In this phase of the drill the second baseman has no glove.

The shortstop tosses the ball to the second baseman, who steps

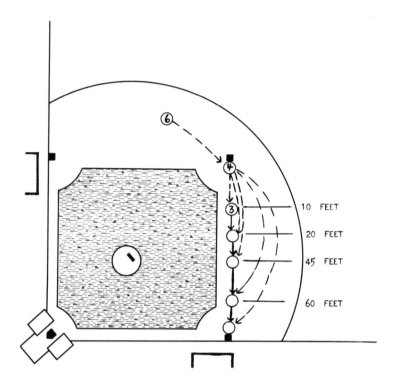

DRILL NO. 147: Detour

on the base with his right foot and lets the ball hit his right hand. He merely keeps the ball moving toward first base—actually a detour of the ball to the first baseman.

B. The first baseman now moves 20 feet away from the bag, and the same drill continues.

C. The first baseman moves 45 feet away from the bag. Continue the drill.

D. The first baseman moves 60 feet away from the bag. The second baseman puts his glove on, and the drill is continued.

E. The first baseman covers first base, and the drill is continued.

148. Alternate Double Play with Runners on First and Third

Purpose

To learn how to get an alternate double play if the usual one is not feasible or cannot be made.

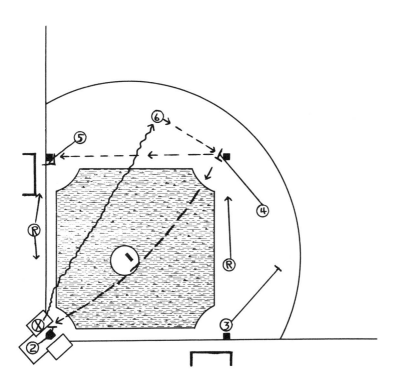

DRILL NO. 148: Alternate Double Play

Procedure

Put runners on first and third, with the infield halfway in, the pitcher on the mound, and the catcher behind the plate. Have balls hit sharply to an infielder or the pitcher. The player fielding the ball "looks" the runner back to third and throws to second base for one out. The runner breaks for home, and the fielder who covered second base throws to the catcher at the plate. The catcher tags the runner for the second out of the double play.

149. Optional Double Play

(See Shortstop Drill No. 159.)

150. Pick-Off Drill

Purpose

To teach the second baseman duties on pick-off plays and to keep the runner close to second base.

Procedure

Put the second baseman and shortstop in position, the pitcher on the mound, and a runner on second base.

A. *Fake Pick-Off.* The pitcher comes set and checks the runner at second. While the pitcher is looking back at the runner, the second baseman makes a short fake to the base. If the runner takes his eyes off the second baseman for a moment, the second baseman can break for the bag. The pitcher turns and throws for the pick-off.

B. *Set Up as in "A" Above.* The shortstop runs for the base. The pitcher, looking at second base, makes no move while the shortstop is out of position. The shortstop then moves between the runner and second base, then back to his position by going toward third base, passing in front of the runner. As the shortstop is even with and directly in front of the runner, the runner probably will move away from the bag with the shortstop. If the runner takes his eyes off the second baseman, the second baseman breaks for the bag as the pitcher pivots and throws to second base for the pick-off.

151. Trailer Play Drill (Special Drill for Cut-Off Plays, Drill No. 40)

Purpose

For protection on over-throws or bad throws to the relay man.

Procedure

When working Drill No. 40 on extra base hits, the shortstop goes out for the relay throw, and the second baseman lines up 25 to 30 feet behind him for protection on bad throws from the outfield. When the second baseman goes out for the relay, the shortstop is the trailer. Second base is being covered by the first baseman, as in Drill No. 135.

152. Pop Fly Drill

(Note Team Drill No. 37.)

CHAPTER 11

SHORTSTOP

DRILLS

The opinion is often expressed that a team must be strong "down the middle." A weak shortstop results in a weak team. He should have a strong arm and be able to make plays to his left, right, and moving in toward the ball.

Since the majority of double plays start at shortstop, he can make or break the second baseman. A good team will average a double play per game and will complete a double play in less than five seconds from the crack of the bat until the first baseman catches the ball.

Designed to strengthen the shortstop's arm, to help teach him to be in the right place and make the right play, especially the all-important double play, the following drills should play a big part in the success of the infield.

153. Check-List for Proper Execution

(Note Screening Candidates Drill No. 207.)

154. Fielding and Throwing

Purpose

To orient the shortstop for all throws to all bases.

Procedure

Place the shortstop in his fielding position and hit balls to his right, left, and straight at him. Be sure to hit both hard and slow balls.

A. *Throws to First Base.* He fields the ball with his left foot in front of his right. If the ball is hit slowly and straight at him, he scoops the ball outside his left foot, and throws in one motion. On a fast rolling ball the ball is fielded directly in front of his body.

On balls to his right, the shortstop will go over to his right, and just as the ball is hitting his glove, he sets his right foot for sliding on the inside of his foot, plants this foot, and then throws without a further step.

On balls to his left, he fields them and pivots his right foot around behind his left, plants his right foot and throws.

B. *Throws to Third Base.* With a runner on second base, on balls hit directly to the shortstop and to his right, the third baseman covers third. The shortstop makes the throw without a step, with a clockwise pivot of the body, and knee high to the third baseman.

C. *Throws to Second Base.* (Note Drill No. 157.)

D. *Throws to Home Plate.* Hit both hard and slow balls to the shortstop. He should charge and field the ball, then throw overhand, if possible, knee high to the catcher.

E. *Throws on Relays.* The shortstop goes out for relay throws from left field, left center, and center field. He receives the ball head high on the glove side, moving toward the base at which he is going to throw. The throw is directly overhand, and in most cases it is a one-hop long bounce. Crow-hop step is used to make the throw.

155. Receiving Throws

Purpose

To help the shortstop learn the correct position and how to handle all throws.

Procedure

A. *Throws from the Pitcher When Fielding Batted Balls:*
Put the pitcher on the mound and the shortstop in his fielding

position. Hit ground balls to the pitcher, who whirls and throws to the shortstop covering second base for a force-out or to start a double play.

B. *Throws from the Catcher:*

1. On an attempted steal of second base, the shortstop breaks for second on the pitch, and the catcher throws to the shortstop covering second. After this is practiced a few times, put a runner on first base and have him break for second on the pitch.

2. The attempted double steal. Work first without runners, then with runners on first and third bases.

The pitcher delivers the ball to the catcher, who throws to the shortstop, who is three feet in front of second base, toward the mound. Moving in to meet the ball, the shortstop cuts off the throw and throws to the catcher knee high. On some throws, the shortstop pivots back and tags the runner at second.

With runners on base, the shortstop must determine whether to make the tag or to cut off the ball and throw home for the tag at the plate. The second baseman can help by telling him, "Home!" or by saying nothing if the runner stays on third base.

C. *Throws from Outfield:*

(Note Drill No. 154-E.)

156. Bunting Situations—Covering Second Base

Purpose

To teach the shortstop to be in the proper position for all bunting plays.

Procedure

Put the first baseman, second baseman, shortstop and pitcher in their respective positions. Have a player or coach bunt the ball.

A. When the ball is bunted with a runner on first base, the second baseman covers first, and the shortstop covers second base. The shortstop covers second for the possible steal or force-out.

B.

1. With runners on first and second bases, the shortstop takes a position near second, holds the runner on, and fakes him

back when he tries to take a lead. He must be certain not to break toward second base as the pitcher is delivering the ball.

2. With runners on first and second bases, the shortstop takes a deep fielding position, giving the runner a lot of room. The shortstop breaks for second base until he notes the runner is breaking back to the bag. The pitcher, who has been looking at second, makes a three-quarter speed perfect strike pitch to the hitter as the shortstop changes direction and charges to cover third base. The third baseman, pitcher, and first baseman cover the bunted ball. Whoever fields the ball throws to the shortstop who is on third base facing the throw.

157. Double Play with the Shortstop as the Starter

Purpose

To give the shortstop the knowledge, timing, and balance necessary to complete a double play.

Procedure

The coach hits balls both hard and slow to the shortstop in the following positions. (The balls thrown by the shortstop should be firm and chest high.)

A. *Balls Hit to the Left, Behind the Bag.* The shortstop attempts to get around the ball in a better position to make the throw to second base. The ball is taken from the glove and thrown as described in Drill No. 145-B for the second baseman. It is a backhand throw.

B. *Balls Hit to the Right.* The shortstop should attempt to get around the ball with his feet in position. The right foot should be forward of the left. This is done to open up the hips so that the second baseman can see the throw coming. The shortstop should make an overhand throw whenever possible.

C. *Balls Hit Directly at the Shortstop.* After moving in to field this ball, the shortstop should plant his feet parallel or his right foot slightly ahead of the left. He then throws the ball overhand to the second baseman.

D. *Balls Hit Near Second Base.* In this case, the shortstop should move over to field the ball and make an underhand throw while still moving forward toward second base. The toss should be firm and hard so that the ball does not hang in the air.

158. Double Play with the Shortstop as the Middleman

Purpose

To acquaint the shortstop with all possible ways to receive throws and make the pivots to complete the double play.

Procedure

The coach hits ground balls to the second baseman and other in-fielders, who throw to the shortstop; he receives the ball and makes the following plays:

A. *Pivot Steps:*

1. Right foot drag:
   The shortstop runs toward the bag, and places his right foot just short of the bag before or after receiving the ball. He then steps with his left foot and drags his right foot across the bag for the out. After dragging his right foot across the bag, he plants it behind his left and throws off his right foot.
2. Right foot planted on the bag:
   If the shortstop has time, he can receive the ball, plant his right foot on the bag, and throw from that position. His forward follow-through carries him up the base line.
3. Left foot and pivot:
   Moving across the bag, the shortstop hits it with his left foot, pivots to his right behind the left, and plants it to make the throw. His momentum should carry him toward right field, out of the way of the runner.
4. Tags bag with left foot and pivots right:
   The shortstop moves to the bag and takes the throw on the side nearest the mound. He tags the bag with his left foot and steps toward the mound to his right foot to complete the throw.
5. Receiving the ball behind the bag:
   When a ball is hit to either the first or second baseman on the

line, the shortstop assumes a position three to four feet behind the bag and lines up the throw. As he is receiving the ball, he takes a small crow-hop to his right foot, stepping on the bag with his left as he throws. His momentum from the throw and a jump off the left leg carries him up and over the sliding runner. The ball is actually thrown before the jump is made.

B. *Receiving Throws from the Second Baseman:*

The shortstop gets to the bag as quickly as possible, moving directly toward the ball, and tries to receive the ball chest high. Actually, time and practice will tell where he likes to receive the ball.

C. *Receiving Throws from the Pitcher:*

The coach hits balls to the pitcher, who whirls and throws chest high to the shortstop. The shortstop should be straddling the bag, waiting for the throw just in back of the bag, or be on the third base side. He then makes the best pivot to complete the play.

D. *Receiving Throws from the Catcher:*

This throw will result from either a bunt or a swinging bunt. The catcher throws chest high to the shortstop, and the play is completed in the same manner as Drill "C" above.

E. *Receiving Throws from the First Baseman:*

(Described in Drill A-5 above.)

F. *Timing the Double Play:*

With a stop watch, time the double play from the crack of the bat until the first baseman receives the ball. The elapsed time should be between 3.5 and 4.5 seconds.

159. Optional Double Play Drill with Runners on First and Second Bases

Purpose

To teach the shortstop and other infielders to try for a different double play if the original play cannot be carried out.

Procedure

Have the infield in the double play position. Place runners on first and second bases, and hit a slow roller to one of the infielders. The infielder playing the ball throws to second for the first out. When it is obvious that the ball was hit so slowly that the second out cannot be

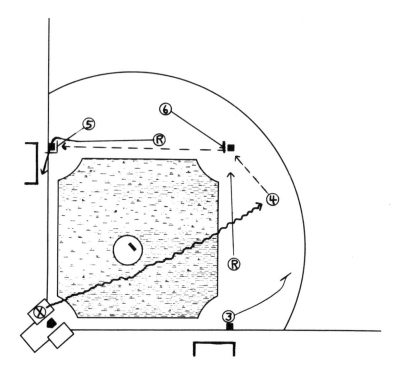

DRILL NO. 159: Optional Double Play

made at first, the shortstop or second baseman covering second throws the ball to third in an attempt to catch the runner off the bag in case he has rounded third base. This throw should be made without hesitation, because looking first and then throwing would be too late.

160. Alternate Double Play

(Note Second Base Drill No. 148.)

161. Pick-Off Drill

Purpose

To help the shortstop and other players master the pick-off play and to help them learn to keep the runner "honest."

Procedure

Use the shortstop in position, pitcher on the mound, catcher behind the plate, and a runner on second base.

A. *Count System.* The pitcher receives the pick-off sign from the shortstop prior to getting on the rubber. He then sees the call of a pitch-out from the catcher. He now assumes a set stance and looks at the runner on second base.

As soon as the pitcher turns his head toward home, the shortstop breaks for second base. When the pitcher looks toward home, he starts counting "one–two–" and on "three" he whirls to his glove side and throws knee high to the shortstop covering second base.

B. *Another Count System.* After the pitcher gets his sign from the catcher, and is in his set stance, he does not look toward the shortstop, but continues to look toward the catcher and begins his stretch. When the ball meets the glove, chest high, the shortstop breaks for second base. The pitcher starts his count at the same time and again on "three" he throws to the shortstop at second base.

C. *Daylight System.* After the pitcher receives the signs, he assumes set stance on the rubber, and looks back to the shortstop, who breaks for second base. When the pitcher sees daylight between the shortstop and the runner, he looks toward home, pivots toward his glove side, and throws to the shortstop at second base.

162. Special Drill for Fielding Balls in the Hole— Shortstop's Right

Purpose

To teach the shortstop how to field balls and throw them when they are hit in the hole. This drill also helps to strengthen the shortstop's arm.

Procedure

The shortstop is in a position directly in line with a ball hit in the hole. Place the shortstop on the edge of the infield grass. The coach rolls balls to him. The shortstop fields the ball, comes up with it, and throws to first base without taking a stride. His left shoulder is facing

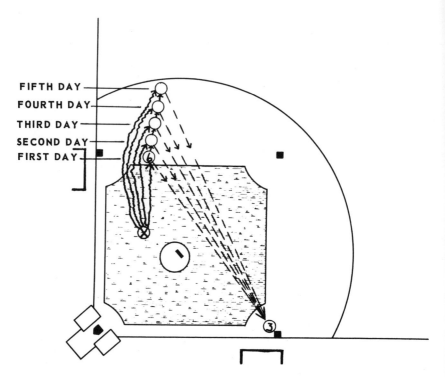

DRILL NO. 162: Special Drill for Shortstop in the Hole

first base. His pivot foot is well behind his other foot. His legs are spread wide. In two weeks he should throw from the *outfield* grass.

The shortstop should work at this no more than 10 minutes for a period of three days; that is, ten minutes per day. On the second day he should be moved back 10 feet behind where he worked the first day, and on the third day he should be moved back 10 feet farther.

163. Teamwork with Third Baseman

Purpose

To teach the shortstop to work with the third baseman.

Procedure

A. Ground Ball Between Third Base and Shortstop. With the shortstop and third baseman in fielding position, the coach hits ground balls between them at all speeds.

If the shortstop knows that he can field the ball and make the play to first base, he yells, "I got it; I got it!" Otherwise, the third baseman takes every ball.

B. Runner on Second Base Only. Have the runner on second base run to third at the crack of the bat. The coach should have hit the ball in the hole to the right of the shortstop, who fields the ball and throws the runner out at third.

C. Relay and Pitch Called by the Catcher. With the shortstop and the third baseman in position, the shortstop sees the pitch called by the catcher. By the use of a sign or voice the shortstop tells the third baseman which pitch is being thrown, especially if the pitch is a change-up and a right handed hitter is at bat.

The coach should go through this drill until the players involved have mastered it and he is certain that the opposing team cannot read it.

164. Trailer Play Drill

(Note Second Base Drill No. 151.)

165. Pop Fly Drill

(Note Team Drill No. 37.)

Since the third base position is the hot corner, the third baseman needs drills to help him develop fast reflexes. He needs sure, fast hands and an accurate arm. Although his throws need not all be hard, they may have to be made from any position. He must be able to get in front of the ball, knock it down if necessary, and throw the runner out.

The purpose of the following drills is to make a better third baseman out of any player with good hands.

CHAPTER *12*

THIRD BASEMAN

DRILLS

166. Check-List for Proper Execution

(Note Screening Candidates Drill No. 207.)

167. In-Place Reach and Field Drill

(Note First Baseman Drill No. 126 and Gimmick No. 239.)

168. Fielding Bunts

Purpose

To teach the third baseman how to field bunts of all types.

Procedure

Place the following players in their defense positions: third baseman, second baseman, first baseman, pitcher, and catcher.

The coach assumes a position near home plate and rolls the ball to the third baseman, who throws the ball to the first or second baseman. The third baseman covers third for the force-out on throws from the pitcher or catcher. In fielding bunts the third baseman must take a path to the ball which will give him good position for throwing.

A. *Fast Roll.* When the ball is rolling fast, the third baseman charges the ball, fields it with his glove, then makes his throw to the proper base. This bunt can sometimes be thrown to second base for an attempted double play or force-out.

B. *Slow Roll.* The third baseman charges the ball and picks it up with his bare hand by letting the ball roll into a cupped relaxed hand. He then takes a firm throwing grip and throws it to first base only.

C. *Ball That Stopped Rolling.* Place several balls one foot apart half-way between home and third, perpendicular to the foul line, on

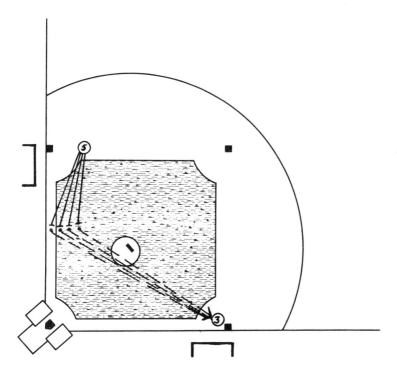

DRILL NO. 168-C: Fielding Bunt That Has Stopped Rolling

the infield grass. The third baseman starts on the base path between second and third and charges the balls. He picks up all balls, one at a time, beginning with the one on the extreme left, and throws them to the first baseman. Generally a crow-hop is used to throw the ball.

The pick-up and throw is made by pushing the ball into the grass with the thumb, index finger, and middle finger in a gripping position. The palm faces the ball as the hand goes down for the pick-up. Depending on practice, the ball can be picked up to the right of either foot. If it is picked up to the right of the right foot, it is thrown from there. If it is picked up to the right of the left foot, the ball is thrown as soon as the right foot hits the ground on the next stride.

D. *Bunt with a Runner on Second Base.* Both the pitcher and the third baseman break for the ball. When the pitcher and the third baseman see that the pitcher can field the ball, and the third baseman hears the pitcher yell, "I have it!" he breaks back for the bag to take the throw from the pitcher. He fields the ball in the manner of a first baseman.

If the third baseman sees that the pitcher cannot get the ball, he continues his charge and makes the play to first base as described in the drill above. He should also yell, "I have it!"

169. Throwing Fielded Bunts

Purpose

To teach the third baseman the quickest or best throw to a base in a variety of ways.

Procedure

Place the catcher, first baseman, second baseman, and third baseman in their respective positions. Roll balls that will stop, fast-rolling balls, and some that are slow to the third baseman.

A. *Throw to Home.* The throws home are usually made when the third baseman has charged the ball. Since this is the case, and because most of these throws have to be made quickly, the throw is made underhand from the fielding position.

B. *Throw to First Base.* This throw is always made when the third baseman has charged the ball. The throw usually is made underhand or side-arm. The third baseman should get into fielding position with the left shoulder pointing diagonally toward first base before fielding the ball. Throws can be made with a crow-hop or directly from the position of the feet when the ball is fielded.

C. *Throw to Second Base.* As the third baseman charges the ball, he works into position so that his chest faces first base and his left shoulder points diagonally toward second base. He fields the ball in his glove and throws overhand or three-quarters, chest high, to second base. This play should be made only on hard bunted balls.

170. Fielding and Throwing Batted Balls

Purpose

To teach the third baseman the necessary fundamentals to make all throws to all bases.

Procedure

Place all infielders in position. The coach hits balls to the third baseman, who throws to the bases as follows:

A. *To First Base.* Balls are hit to the third baseman's left, right, and directly at him. Some are hit hard and some slowly. When he charges the slow ball, he usually has to make an underhand or side-arm throw. On balls hit to his left, he will make a three-quarter to a side-arm throw. And he will throw directly overhand on balls hit straight at him and to his right.

B. *To Second Base.* With the exception of the slowly hit ball, all other balls fielded should be thrown overhand to the second baseman.

C. *To Home.* All throws should be overhand when possible, the exception being the slowly hit ball.

D. *Relay Cut-Off Man with Runners in Scoring Position.* On balls hit to left field or to left center, the third baseman assumes a position on the infield grass between the mound and third base, lining up the throw from the outfield to the catcher. If the throw is not in line with the catcher, or the catcher yells, "Cut it!" the third baseman cuts it off and either relays it to the catcher or some other base.

171. Teamwork with the Shortstop

A. *Ground Balls Between Shortstop and Third Base.* (Note Shortstop Drill No. 163-A.)

B. *With Runner on Second and a Ground Ball in the Hole to Right of Shortstop.* (Note Shortstop Drill No. 163-B.)

C. *Relay of Pitch Called for by Catcher.* (Note Shortstop Drill No. 163-C.)

172. Receiving Throws on Batted Balls

Purpose

To teach the third baseman how to cover third base and receive the ball for tags or force-outs.

Procedure

Have fielders in position and roll or hit balls to the following:

A. *Catcher—for a tag play.* The third baseman straddles the bag and receives the throw from the catcher. He makes the tag as described in Drill No. 143-E.

On a force-out, the third baseman assumes a position on the side of the bag nearest to the catcher and tags the bag with the right foot. He should be ready for a possible throw to first base for a double play.

B. *Pitcher.* Assumes the same position as when receiving throws from the catcher.

C. *First Baseman.* The same as the above.

D. *Outfield.* The third baseman straddles the bag and faces the outfielder or the relay man making the throw.

E. *Shortstop.* (Drill No. 163-B.)

173. Pick-Off Play

Purpose

To teach the third baseman how to hold the runner close to the base or to pick him off.

Procedure

Put a runner on third base with the pitcher, catcher, and third baseman in position.

A. *Pitcher:*

    1. The pitcher uses the count system. In a wind-up stance, he gets the pitch sign from the catcher. The pitcher looks toward third, and when he looks toward home, the third baseman breaks for the bag and straddles it. The pitcher counts "one" and on "two" turns in a clockwise motion and throws knee high to third base. The third baseman and the pitcher have a prearranged signal for the pick-off.

    2. The pitcher is in a set stance. He gets his sign, looks at third, to home, counts "one" and on "two" throws to third base. The third baseman breaks when the pitcher turns his head from third to home.

B. *Catcher:*

The catcher gives a pitch-out sign to the pitcher and a pick-off sign to the third baseman. When the ball is 10 to 15 feet in front of home plate, the third baseman breaks for third. He stands on the infield side of the bag, but not straddling it. The catcher throws the ball about two or three feet on the infield side of the bag. This prevents his hitting the runner with the ball.

174. Pop Fly Drill

(Note Team Drill No. 37.)

CHAPTER *13*

OUTFIELD DRILLS

here is more to playing the outfield than catching a fly ball. If an outfielder misses a ball, the runner takes extra bases. However, if an infielder misses one, the runner may be held to a single by an aggressive outfielder, and there is a chance of a double play or a force-out. An outfielder must see how many plays he can get into on every ball hit. Nothing looks better than to see an outfielder backing up an over-throw or making a put-out in a rundown play. An outfielder is never a good outfielder until he can field ground balls, line drives, balls hit over his head, and make low hard throws.

Not only should the following drills improve an outfielder's skills, but they should also make him believe he is a large part of the game, and was not put in the outfield because he is the poorest player on the team.

175. Check-List for Proper Execution

(Note Screening Candidates Drill No. 207.)

176. Touch Grass— Right and Left Drill

(Note General Infield Drill No. 117.)

177. Equilibrium Drill

(Note General Infield Drill No. 119 and repeat.)

178. Toe-Running Drill

Purpose

To teach outfielders to run on their toes and to adjust their eyes to seeing a ball while the player is running.

Procedure

When the outfielder is doing his extra running, he should focus his eyes on a spot or small object the size of a baseball, such as the insulator on a light pole. All of his running should be done up on his toes in order to prevent bouncing. If the object upon which he has his eyes focused seems to be bouncing, the fielder probably is running on his heels.

179. Ground Ball Drill

Purpose

To teach the outfielders how to block a ball and how to field various ground balls.

Procedure

Outfielders should get around all balls, if it is at all possible, to get into position to throw the ball.

The coach hits ground balls to the outfielders telling them whether there is a play to make or not.

A. *With no play.* The outfielder's job is to get the ball into second base, but above all to keep it from getting past him. When the coach hits the ball, the outfielder charges it until he gets 12 to 15 feet in front of the ball. If the ball takes a good hop and he can time it correctly, he fields the ball with two hands as an infielder, moving in and catching the ball, then crow-hopping as he throws to second base. If the ball is rolling and not bouncing, the outfielder goes down on the knee of his throwing side, 15 feet in front of the ball. A right handed outfielder goes down on his right knee, his left foot is parallel to his knee, and his right leg is extended out to his right, not directly behind him. A left handed outfielder goes down on his left knee and the positions are reversed. However, both keep their shoulders perpendicular to the path of the ball. Then, using a crow-hop, the outfielder fields the ball, comes up with it, and throws to second base.

B. *With a base runner and a play to make.* The outfielder charges the ball hard until he is 12 to 15 feet in front of it; then he begins to take short choppy steps as a football player does as he is about to make a tackle. If the ball takes a true hop, he fields it with two hands, takes a crow-hop and throws to the base required. If the ball is not hopping, but rolling, the outfielder makes a one-hand glove pick-up of the ball, preferably on the glove side. It is fielded easier on the outside of the foot.

C. *Infield work.* For ground ball work, the coach should put the outfielders on the infield and give them daily work in early season practice and all season.

180. Fly Ball Practice

Purpose

To give outfielders practice on all types of fly balls.

Procedure

The coach hits fly balls to the outfielder without telling him where the ball is going to be hit.

A. *Position for Throwing.* As in the ground ball drill, the outfielder must get around the ball to be in position for throwing to the proper base.

B. *Line Drives.* For practice on the line drive, these balls should be hit very sharply and directly at the outfielder.

C. *Balls Hit Directly over the Fielder's Head.* Bring the outfielder in and hit lazy fly balls directly over his head. The right-hander pivots clockwise, to his right, and as he goes back, he runs in an arc to his right while looking at the ball. When he receives it, his glove hand will be facing the ball and he will be in good position to throw. The left handed player breaks in the opposite direction.

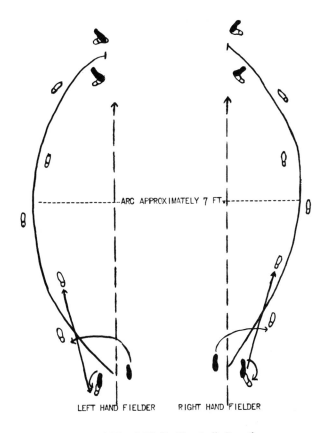

LEFT HAND FIELDER   RIGHT HAND FIELDER

DRILL NO. 180-C: Fly Ball Practice

D. Balls Hit to the Fielder's Right. Breaking to his right, the fielder goes back and around the ball as he gets in position to throw before making the catch.

E. Balls Hit to the Fielder's Left. The fielder breaks left and back while getting in position to throw.

F. Short Fly Balls in Front of Fielder. The fielder breaks in for the ball and decides either to catch or block it. For practice, do not let the fielder hold up on the ball, but make him come through on it. If the ball is low, he should catch it one-handed. If the ball cannot be caught, the outfielder keeps his arm down and out in front of his legs, glove perpendicular to the ground, fingers down, facing the ball. He remains in this position with neither a sweep nor a slap of the glove downward. His job is to keep the ball in front of him.

181. Playing the Ball in the Sun

Purpose

To teach players to play the ball in the sun with or without sun glasses.

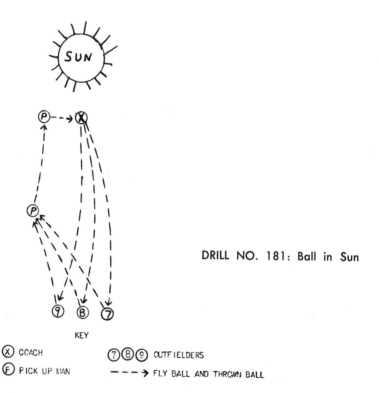

DRILL NO. 181: Ball in Sun

KEY

Ⓧ COACH   ⑦⑧⑨ OUTFIELDERS
Ⓟ PICK UP MAN   - - -→ FLY BALL AND THROWN BALL

Procedure

Put outfielders in position so that all fungoed balls will be directly in the sun for the fielders. The sun should be behind the hitter's back. Fungo balls will simulate actual hitting in a game situation.

ILLUS. NO. 25: An outfielder shields his eyes from the sun with his glove.
(See Drill No. 181.)

A. *Without Sun Glasses or if the Sun Is Directly Behind the Hitter:*

Outfielders should attempt to play hitters to their strong side. As an example, a right fielder would play a left handed pull hitter closer to the right field foul line than he normally would. While the pitch is being made and the batter is ready to hit, the outfielder shields his eyes from the sun with his glove. When the ball is hit, he attempts to keep his glove in this position as long as possible. He then attempts to get his body in position so that he is not looking directly into the sun when he catches the ball. (Note Illustration No. 25, page 157.)

B. *With Sun Glasses:*

Keeping his glove in the position described above, the outfielder plays the hitter to his power side. Waiting until he knows exactly where the ball is, he then flips his glasses down and makes the catch. Flipping the glasses too early will cause the outfielder to lose the ball or misjudge it.

Playing in the sun and using the sun glasses requires extra practice.

182. Catching Fly Balls at the Fence

Purpose

To teach outfielders how to catch fly balls at or near the fence.

Procedure

Place the outfielder 10 to 12 feet from the fence. Throw fly balls to the fence, so that the outfielder will have to run back to the fence and jump to catch the ball.

Have the outfielder approach the fence by getting to it as quickly as possible and feeling for it with his hand or glove while keeping his eye on the ball. After getting to the fence, the outfielder should turn his body sideways before jumping for the ball. Outfielders should not be permitted to back up to the fence before jumping, since this position often causes them to hit the fence with their buttocks, resulting in loss of balance and failure to catch the ball.

183. Fence Drills

Purpose

To teach outfielders how to go to the fence and play a ball and to teach them how to play balls off the fence.

Procedure

The coach hits or throws balls to the outfielders at or near the fence. He tries to give the outfielders all possible plays around the fence. A relay man should be placed to receive the throws.

A. *Balls Lying Against the Fence:*

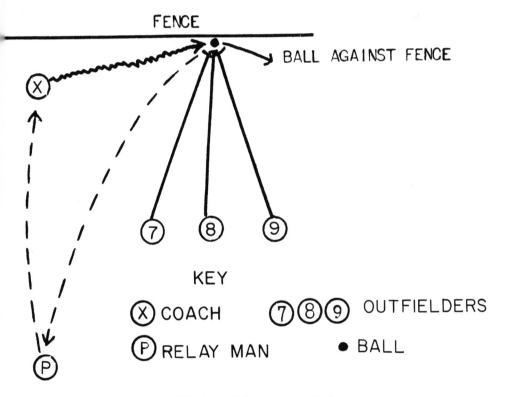

DRILL NO. 183-A: Ball Lying Against Fence

Place balls against the fence, and put the outfielders 25 to 30 feet away from the fence. Have the outfielders approach the ball from all angles and throw to a relay man. Right-handers should pick up the ball with their right foot on the right side of the ball, and left-handers should pick up the ball with their left foot on the left side of the ball without straddling it. The throw should begin directly from where the outfielder picks up the ball. As he picks it up, he should crow-hop and throw to a relay man.

B. *Ball Rebounding from a Fence:*

Hit balls against the fence at different angles for outfielders, who play the ball off the fence and throw to a relay man.

C. *Crashing the Fence:*

The outfielder gets approximately 15 feet from the fence, and the coach throws balls so that they can be caught by the outfielder if he jumps high up against the fence. As the ball is thrown, the outfielder breaks to the fence as fast as possible and puts his foot and leg that are nearest the wall up against the fence, using them to take up the shock and to aid in climbing the wall. He should keep his eye on the ball as much as possible. He may take his eye off the ball just as he hits the fence. (Note Illustration No. 26, page 161.)

184. Throwing to Bases

Purpose

To teach outfielders how to throw properly to bases.

Procedure

Hit all types of balls to an outfielder, and have him throw to different bases. He should make a direct overhand throw that takes one long bounce to the base. The outfielder should use a crow-hop to get something on the ball and for accuracy.

In order to get rid of the ball as quickly as possible, with maximum power in the throw, the outfielder should, if possible, time his catch so that the ball hits his glove just a fraction of a second before his pivot foot (foot on throwing side) hits the ground. He then crow-hops to that foot and fires the ball. Naturally, he should be moving forward toward the ball and the base to which he is making the throw.

ILLUS. NO. 26: An outfielder "climbing the wall" to field a long fly ball.
(See Drill No. 183.)

185. Faking a Throw to a Base for a Pick-Off

Purpose

To teach outfielders how to fake a throw to a base and catch a runner off another base.

Procedure

Place defensive players in position and hit ground ball singles to the outfield. Put the runners on base and have them make big turns.

A. *Right Fielder*. The ball is hit to right field, between the first and second basemen. A runner goes to first base and makes a big turn. The catcher follows the runner and covers first base. The pitcher backs up the catcher, while the first and second basemen go out toward right field on ground balls in that area. The right fielder charges the ball, picks it up, and makes a motion toward second base. He immediately whirls and throws to the catcher covering first base.

B. *Center Fielder with a Runner on First Base*. The ball is hit to center field. The runner rounds second base. Then the center fielder fakes a throw to third, but whirls and throws to second base.

C. *Left Fielder*. Repeat as for center fielder.

A throw behind the runner is never made from a deep position.

186. Hitting the Cut-Off and Relay Men

Purpose

To teach outfielders how to make the throw for a perfect relay.

Procedure

Place all outfielders and infielders in their proper positions. Hit to all positions in the outfield, and have outfielders make all plays where outfielders throw to the infield or relay man.

A. With a quick, snappy motion, the outfielders throw to the relay man, hitting him on the glove side, head high. The crow-hop may not be necessary on the shorter throws. (Drill No. 40)

B. Using the crow-hop, the outfielder makes a hard overhand throw to the cut-off man. The ball is thrown so that it will take one long hop to the base and will hit the cut-off man's glove above his head. (Drill No. 39)

187. Bunting Situations—Covering Bases

Purpose

To teach the outfielders duties other than catching ground and fly balls.

Procedure

With the defensive team in position and nobody on base, set up all bunting situations.

A. *Right Fielder.* As soon as the bunter has committed himself to bunt, the right fielder breaks for a position to back up the throw. If the throw is to first base, he goes toward first, and if the throw is to second base, he goes toward second. His first steps, however, should be toward first base. His direction changes with the throw.

B. *Center Fielder.* The center fielder always breaks behind second base to back up all bunt situations.

C. *Left Fielder.* The left fielder backs up either second or third base, depending upon where the throw is made on the bunt. However, he usually breaks for third base, if there are runners on base, to be ready for a possible play at third.

188. Back-Up Plays

Purpose

To teach the outfielder that he has a play to make in every situation.

Procedure

With the defensive team in position, hit ground balls to the outfield.

A. *Backing Up Other Outfielders:*
   1. Balls hit to right field are backed up by the center fielder.
   2. Depending upon the position of the ball in center field, balls hit to this area are backed up by the right or the left fielder.

3. Balls hit to left field are backed up by the center fielder.

4. Back-up plays depend largely on who is closer to the outfielder at the time he is receiving the ball. The other outfielder may be the relay man.

B. *Backing Up Bases:*
1. Right fielder:
   a. The right fielder backs up first base on all throws except throws on balls hit to the right side of the infield. On these plays he backs up the infielders.
   b. The right fielder backs up all throws to second base from the left side of the infield.
2. Center fielder:
   The center fielder backs up second base whenever there is a possible play at that base.
3. Left fielder:
   a. The left fielder backs up second base on all plays to second base from the right side of the infield and, particularly, singles to right field.
   b. The left fielder backs up third base on all possible plays at third base, particularly on singles to right field with a runner on first, and on triples to right.

Outfielders can also get into run-down plays while backing up throws. He should back up the base near the area where the ball would go if it got past the infielder.

189. Outfielder Teamwork Drill

Purpose

To teach outfielders that they need help and should expect and give help to other outfielders.

Procedure

Put the team in defensive positions, and place an imaginary runner or runners on base. Do not tell the outfielder catching the ball where the imaginary runner is located. The coach has this outfielder turn his back while he signals the other outfielders where the runner is stationed.

Signals:

One finger for first base; two fingers for second base; three fingers for third base, and the fist for no runner on base. The coach then tells all outfielders the number of outs and the score.

A. *Ground Balls.* The outfielder nearest the fielder catching the ball tells him where to throw the ball. He tells him this just before he catches the ball.

B. *Fly Balls.* Change the routine above and put an actual runner on third base. The outfielder nearest the fielder making the play tells him whether to throw home or to another base. In this case imaginary runners are on other bases.

190. Duty Drills—Pre-Game

Purpose

To acquaint outfielders with the conditions under which they will play and the opposing team's strengths and weaknesses.

A. *Opposing Team.* When the opposing team takes batting practice, look for their power and the direction the players hit most frequently. Look for speed, and watch their arms for throwing ability. Also look for injuries.

B. *Self-orientation.* The outfielders loosen up their arms by throwing to the bases during infield and outfield practice. While he is in the outfield shagging balls, the outfielder should study the length of the grass, hardness of the ground, position of the sun, the construction of the fence, and its effect upon the ball. Fungo hitters should hit all types of balls, some against the fence, and some near the fence. In a field where the ball may be played in the sun, some balls should be hit into the sun so that the outfielder can become oriented to it.

191. Game Situation Drill

Purpose

To let the outfielders experience as many game situations as possible.

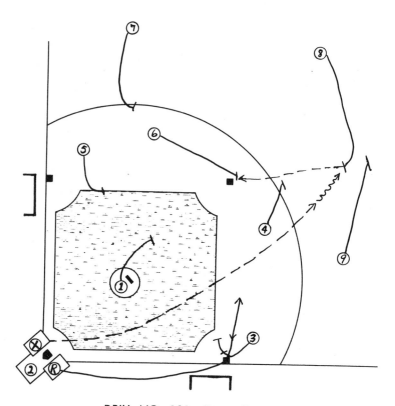

DRILL NO. 191: Game Situation

Procedure

Place a complete defensive ball team on the field. Have extra men and pitchers take their turn at bat. The batter swings the bat, and at that time the coach hits a ball through the infield so that the outfielders make all the plays. To make it realistic, the hitters run the bases. All types of fly and ground balls should be hit, including singles and extra base hits.

Suggested drills to go with this one are the following: Nos. 83, 115, 135, 138-D, 143-C, 154-E, 164, 170-D, 172-D.

CHAPTER 14

BASE-RUNNING
DRILLS

Good base running will keep a ball club winning more than 50 percent of its games. A running club forces the opposition into making errors. A player who knows how to slide wants to slide, and will take the extra base. He will score from second and advance to third from first on most balls hit to centerfield and right field. All players, including pitchers, need sliding and base-running drills.

Sliding directly at a bag is best when stealing. In stealing, most jumps are gotten on the pitcher, but occasionally a player can run on a catcher's poor arm or movements.

Since speed can be increased, running should be taught. Players must run in a relaxed manner, use high knee action, elbows relaxed comfortably close to the body and bent approximately 90 degrees, and should be up on their toes. The toes should point directly ahead and should be placed in front of the nose. The body should lean forward. Exceptions to this body lean and foot placement are on the turns, when the body leans toward the middle of the diamond and forward. The left foot will naturally fall nearer to the inside of the diamond than the right foot.

The following drills on base running are designed to develop players into better base runners.

192. Check-List for Proper Execution

(Note Screening Candidates Drill No. 207.)

193. Break from Home

(Note Drill No. 57.)

194. Rounding Bases

Purpose

To keep runners from going too far out of the base paths while making turns at the bases.

Procedure

When using Drill Nos. 196 and 203, have your players concentrate on their turns. The body should lean toward the infield while rounding bases. Being certain not to break his stride, the base runner should hit the base with either foot. Although some coaches teach that the runner must hit the base with his left foot, and some say the right foot, the important thing is that he hits the base without breaking stride.

A. *First Base:*

1. Have the player run straight for first base until he is 12 to 15 feet from the bag. At this time, he should cross his left foot over his right, making about a three-foot bend in his path before hitting the base.
2. Another method is for the runner to start to bend toward foul territory about halfway to first base, then turn in and touch the base with either foot.

B. *Second Base:*

While rounding and coming from first base, the base runner should have enough bend in his path and lean of his body to make the turn at second. However, if he is coming directly from first base, he should turn as described for first base.

C. *Third Base:*

When rounding and coming from second base, the base runner should have enough bend or arch in his path to make the turn without using the cross-over step. His lead off second base should be taken on the outfield side of the base path instead of on the base line. His turn is similar to that made at first base.

195. Alternate Speed Base-Running Drill

Purpose

To develop players mentally and physically for base running.

Procedure

As a closing drill for a day's work, this will give the necessary running for the day.

A. The team lines up at home plate. Each player stands in the batter's box, swings at an imaginary ball, drops the bat, and breaks for first base at full speed. He jogs to second base, runs full speed to third, and jogs home. Repeat five times.

B. The same start is used as in "A" above. The batter runs full speed to second base and jogs on around to the starting position. Repeat five times.

C. Use the same starting approach. The batter runs full speed to third base and jogs to the starting position. Repeat three times.

D. Using the same starting approach, the batter runs the bases full speed all the way. Repeat twice.

196. Timed Running Practice

Purpose

To get the players conscious of their speed and to want to improve.

Procedure

Time players with a stop watch.

A. Short distance. Have players run 50-yard sprints, and when they are loose, time them.

B. Base running for time. (Note Drill No. 19.)

C. Clock the base runners during the game.

197. Starts and Returns at First Base

Purpose

To teach base runners how to get a better lead at first base, which depends somewhat on the pitcher's moves.

Procedure

Place the pitcher, catcher, and the first baseman in their respective positions. Line the remainder of the players up on the right field foul line, starting with one on first base. Space them three or four feet apart with one foot on the foul line, with the exception of the one player on first, who has one foot on the bag. All players take three good steps perpendicular to the foul line toward second base for a normal lead. Knees should be bent, weight on the balls of the feet, and their eyes on the pitcher. If the pitcher throws home, all players run 10 to 12 steps toward second base.

Players line up again in their original position, take their three-step lead, and return to their starting positions as the pitcher tries to pick the runner off the bag. In their return, they use a right foot cross-over step and one more to hit the bag (or line in this case) with their left foot. This is a two-step procedure with the left foot touching the outside corner of the bag. The right foot pivots back and around toward the right field foul line.

A. *Without Ball.* Have players run through the drill without a ball or a pitcher.

B. *With Ball.* Using a ball in a game-like situation, run through the drill as above.

C. *Individually.* Players work on these basic steps on the side. Use three steps to get off the base and two in getting back on. When the pitcher has good moves, use shorter steps, but the same number. If his moves are just fair, use a fair-sized step, and if his moves are poor, use large steps and perhaps a crow-hop after the third step.

198. Lead-Off Base Drill

Purpose

To teach players how to get a better lead off all bases.

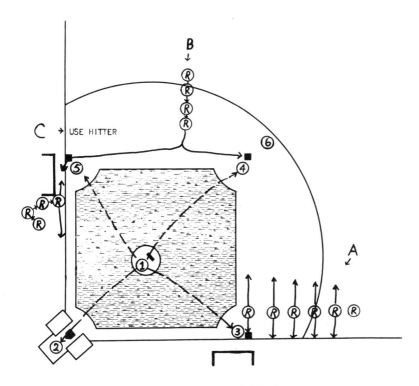

DRILL NO. 198: Lead-Off Base

Procedure

Each player is taken individually and put on base. The pitcher goes through the same motions he would use in a game. If the runner takes too much lead he picks him off. To insure a better start, rock or shuffle on the balls of the feet.

A. *Lead Off First Base.* Teach the lead-off as in Drill No. 197. However, a walking lead may be more desirable for some players. The player starts walking slowly with short steps as the pitcher gets set, and when he throws to the catcher, the runner takes off for second base. His return, however, may have to be a head-first dive.

B. *Lead Off Second Base.* The runner lines up about six feet behind the base line between second and third base and takes a lead that normally would not cause him to get picked off. As the pitcher is looking back at him, the runner takes short, choppy steps while moving toward the pitcher, but at an angle toward third base. By the time the pitch is made, he is almost on the base line with a good lead, if he is going to steal. If he is not going to steal, he does not move up to the base line, but remains behind it to get a better angle for rounding third base. Getting back to second base can be executed by a head-first dive or by a feet-first slide.

C. *Lead Off Third Base.* The runner normally takes three good-sized steps for the lead. On the pitch, he moves toward home, stopping when the ball goes past the batter and returning to third base. Give the runner practice by having the batter hit the ball. If it is a ground ball, the runner breaks for home. If it is a fly ball, he tags up and tries to score. This is a very important phase of the drill.

Runners should be cautioned not to move so fast and far toward home that they will have to return to third when the ball is hit.

199. Sliding Drills—Indoors

Purpose

To learn how to slide during inclement weather. Some teams cannot get outside until a few days before their first game. In this case, sliding should be taught indoors.

Procedure

Use the same approach and sliding techniques as in Drill No. 200. The only exception is the equipment used. For the approach, use a rubber mat, or a gymnastic mat, on the gymnasium floor. For the protection of the body, use pads for the elbows and knees, several pairs of sweat pants, sweat socks on the hands, and stockings on the feet.

200. Sliding Drills—Outdoors

Purpose

To help all players develop skills in the basic slides to the extent that they execute them well, safely, with confidence and enthusiasm.

Basically, sliding is needed to get that extra base, not for the purpose of stealing. These drills should help all players, including pitchers, learn to slide instead of jumping at the bag, a cause of numerous injuries.

Procedure

Lay a bag loose, not tied down, on a spot well covered with grass. Be sure that the ground is not bumpy, and that it does not contain rocks, glass, or other dangerous matter.

Instruct your players to put on old sweat pants over their practice pants. Be sure that they pull off their shoes and run in their stocking feet.

Have beginners go through the motion of sliding on the side of their choice at a slow speed. As they improve, the coach can call for more speed. The coach should supervise all practice.

A. *Straight-in Slide:*

Most beginners want to do this slide, although it is one of the most dangerous since there is little relaxation in the slider as he hits the bag. The first attempt by a beginner may be this slide, although it is not recommended.

The slide is executed by the player half sliding, half jumping at the bag with legs extended straight in front of the slider.

B. *Hook Slide:*

This slide can be made to either side, which should be determined by the position of the fielder and where he moves.

The factors below can serve as a check-list for the coach as he watches players practice the hook slide:

1. Extended foot leaves ground first. It is relaxed and slightly bent.
2. Hooking foot is the take-off foot. It is relaxed and bent.
3. The feet are pushed out in front of the body which goes into nearly a prone position. The soles of the feet never touch the grass or dirt, only the sides of the feet touch.
4. The body is not at right angles to the bag, but angled at about 45 degrees.
5. The slide is on the hip of the extended foot.
6. Hooking foot contacts the bag. This is done with the instep of the inside foot.
7. The body and extended foot are carried away from the bag.

C. Bent Leg Slide:

If there is a need to get up in a hurry, the player may slide into the bag with a bent leg. The momentum of the body and push of the bent leg against the bag will bounce him to his feet. This slide can be made on either side.

1. The extended leg leaves the ground first. However, both feet leave at nearly the same time.
2. The foot of the bent leg comes under the knee of the extended leg.
3. The body is perpendicular to the base.
4. The slide is on the bent leg and hip, mostly on the outside of the calf.
5. The bent leg slides into the bag for the push-up.
6. The extended foot goes to the rear of the bag or beyond, and the slider comes up but remains on the bag.

D. Bent Leg-and-Go Slide:

Although this slide can be executed on either side, the bent left leg is preferable.

1. The right leg leaves the ground first.
2. The foot of the bent leg comes under the knee of the right leg.
3. The body is perpendicular to the base and almost in a sit-up position.
4. The slide is on the calf of the left leg and left hip.
5. The left leg starts the push-up before arriving at the base.
6. The right leg hits the bag for extra push-up.
7. The left leg push-up and the right leg hitting the bag spins the slider so that he is facing the next base with momentum in that direction.

201. Delayed Steal Drills Against Right Handed Pitchers

Purpose

To throw opponents off balance and to keep your team alert for such steals.

Procedure

Place the infield, pitcher, and catcher in position. Also, place runners on first and third bases.

A. *Walk-Off Drill:*

When the pitcher becomes set, the first base runner takes a normal lead. He starts walking when the ball is delivered by the pitcher. When the runner sees or hears the ball hit the catcher's glove, he takes three more walking steps, then breaks at full speed for second base.

B. *Forced Balk:*

1. If the pitcher takes the sign on the rubber and does not look at the first base runner, the base runner breaks for second when the pitcher starts any motion with his hands to go into his stance. This usually happens when his hands are near his thighs.

2. If the pitcher takes the sign off the rubber, he has to look down to see where he places his right foot on the rubber. Then the runner breaks for second base as soon as the pitcher's pivot foot contacts the rubber.

In the above drills, if the first base runner is caught stealing, he should get in a run-down and stay in it as long as possible in order to give the runner on third an opportunity to score if possible.

The runner on third takes such a lead that, if a play is made on him, he will have to dive back to third base to be safe. On the walk-off play, he holds until the catcher throws to second, then breaks for home.

On the forced balk, he holds until the pitcher throws the ball to second. The success of the plays depends upon perfect timing and full speed by the runner on first base.

202. Getting Out of a Run-Down

Purpose

To teach players how to react in a run-down and how to stay in it as long as possible, so that another runner can advance.

Procedure

When using infield run-down Drill No. 120, players should attempt to (1) run into a fielder in the base line without the ball; and

(2) get a player with the ball chasing them at full speed, stop quickly and fall flat on the ground causing the player with the ball to stumble over or miss the base runner, thus giving the base runner a chance to advance to the next base; or (3) attempt to get hit by the ball.

203. Base Coach Drill

Purpose

To teach the base coaches how to handle base runners and to teach the base runners how to look for and listen to the base coaches' signals.

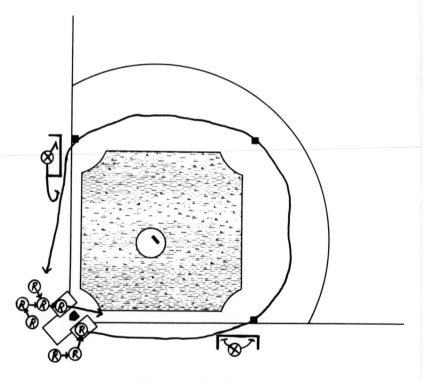

DRILL NO. 203: Base Coach

Procedure

Line up all ball players at home plate. At the slap of the coach's hands, the first runner breaks for first base. Only the first base coach knows where the imaginary ball has been hit. Based upon where the ball has been hit, the first base coach tells the runner what to do—beat it out, make his turn, go for second base, or make his turn and go for two with a slide.

When the runner goes for second, prior to hitting the base, he must look at the third base coach, who is signaling him whether to hold up or go on to third. When the runner comes into third, the coach will tell him to slide, hold up, make his turn, or go on home. The third base coach must listen to the instructions of the first base coach so as not to bring a runner into third who was told to slide.

Pre-game practice must be carried out with real enthusiasm. By scaring the other team in practice, some games are won. A catcher, for instance, by showing his arm, can keep the opposition from stealing. Outfielders can keep them from tagging up and advancing on fly balls or scoring from second on a single.

The umpires should be advised to report to the field one-half hour before game time. This allows time for delays in transportation and prevents a late start. GAMES MUST START ON TIME!

CHAPTER *15*

PRE-GAME
PRACTICE

204. Pre-Game Batting Practice

Purpose

To give each team an equal amount of organized batting practice.

Procedure

Make a time schedule, starting with the time of the game, and work backward from game time. In the schedule allow enough time for: visiting team batting—30 minutes; home team batting—30 minutes; visiting team infield and outfield practice—10 minutes; home team infield and outfield practice—10 minutes; groundskeeping—10 minutes.

During batting practice, someone should hit fungos to the infielders and outfielders. Caution should be used in hitting to the infielders. Do not hit fungos at the same time pitched balls are hit. Hit fungos between pitches.

All extra men should take three swings at the beginning of batting practice. Following them, the starting lineup should start a round of one bunt and four swings each. If time permits, let them continue one bunt and four swings on a second round. If a few minutes are left, do some hit-and-run practice by giving each batter one pitch only.

For faster batting practice use a pitcher who can throw perfect strikes and a catcher.

Below is a sample time schedule of pre-game practice for a 3:30 game. Since the visitors are normally free earlier than the home team, the visitors should take their hitting practice first. However, if they have a late arrival time they should notify the home team coach, and his team can reverse the order of hitting and fielding practice.

2:00——Visiting team batting

2:30——Home team batting

3:00——Visiting team infield and outfield practice

3:10——Home team infield and outfield practice

3:20——Groundskeeper prepares the field for the game

3:25——Umpires and coaches discuss ground rules. Home team coach presents his lineup card to plate umpire first, then the visiting team coach presents his lineup card

3:30——Game time

205. Infield-Outfield Practice

Purpose

To have a well-organized pre-game practice for infielders and outfielders.

Procedure

While the home team is taking batting practice, the visiting team, which has finished its batting practice, starts warming up on the side. This is ten minutes before they take the field, which is thirty minutes before game time. As soon as the home team completes batting practice, the visitors charge to their positions. The coach, with four balls, assumes a position near the mound and hits to the outfielders, who make several throws to the following bases: The left fielder throws to second base and home; the center fielder and the right fielder throw to third and home. A fungo hitter then hits to the outfield for fly ball practice. This hitting should be done from a position just outside the foul lines beyond first and third bases. From these positions there is no danger to infielders, who are taking infield practice as the coach hits balls to them. While the visiting team is taking infield practice the home team is loosening up for their practice, which is taken in the same manner. The home team practice stops ten minutes before game time, and the groundskeeper uses this time in preparing the field for the game.

206. Pitcher Warm-Up Drill

Purpose

To give the starting pitcher ample time to get ready for the game.

A. *Home Team.* Twenty minutes before game time have the pitcher do some type of loosening up exercise. Ten to fifteen minutes before game time, depending upon the weather and the individual, the pitcher should begin to throw. Starting easily, he should gradually increase his speed until he feels loose. Then he should throw his curve and fast ball. Once he feels loose enough, he should work up a sweat, gauging his time so that he will not be warm too long before game time. He will need a few minutes' rest prior to going out on the mound—long enough to wipe off the sweat and get a drink of water. Never rest longer than five minutes.

B. *Visiting Team.* This should be the same as above, except that the pitcher should begin warming up five minutes later, since his team will bat first. This gives him at least five minutes extra in which to warm up. If he gets loose at the same time as the home pitcher, he may have to sit around in the dugout while his team hits. He could cool off too much to be effective in the first inning. He, too, needs a little time on the bench prior to going out on the mound. It is not advisable to rest more than five minutes.

All coaches have new players report to them for practice. Often there are too many to include with the regular players. So a special screening or tryout day is assigned for these players. With this drill call, new candidates can be checked for their ability to make the team. The check-list can also be used.

For players on the team, we have a coach's check-list covering all positions. He can check the progress of each player from spring training through the entire season. If a player has trouble it would be wise to use the check-list to help spot and correct the trouble.

CHAPTER 16

SCREENING
CANDIDATES

207. Coach's Check-List

Grade: A–Excellent
B–Good
C–Fair
D–Poor

Player's Progress:
(1) Beginning of Season
(2) Middle of Season
(3) End of Season

Batting

(1)	(2)	(3)	
___	___	___	1. Knows strike zone
___	___	___	2. Strides correctly
___	___	___	3. Hitches, yet hits well
___	___	___	4. Swings level
___	___	___	5. Has proper hip action
___	___	___	6. Rolls wrists on swing
___	___	___	7. Has good follow-through

Batting

(1)   (2)   (3)

——   ——   ——   8. Never guesses
——   ——   ——   9. Steps toward pitch
——   ——   ——   10. Keeps elbows away from body
——   ——   ——   11. Can hit curve
——   ——   ——   12. Can hit change of speeds
——   ——   ——   13. Can hit fast ball
——   ——   ——   14. Can hit behind runner or opposite field
——   ——   ——   15. Not afraid of pitched ball
——   ——   ——   16. Bends knees slightly prior to pitch
——   ——   ——   17. Starts swing at proper time
——   ——   ——   18. Has proper grip on bat
——   ——   ——   19. Is relaxed at plate
——   ——   ——   20. Weight on balls of feet
——   ——   ——   21. Keeps both eyes level and on the ball
——   ——   ——   22. Takes signs easily

Bunting

——   ——   ——   1. Bat parallel with ground
——   ——   ——   2. Angle of bat is good
——   ——   ——   3. Bunts from front end of batter's box
——   ——   ——   4. Can bunt toward first
——   ——   ——   5. Can bunt toward third
——   ——   ——   6. Always bunts strikes
——   ——   ——   7. Commits himself to bunt at proper time
——   ——   ——   8. Carries bat shoulder high
——   ——   ——   9. Weight on balls of feet
——   ——   ——   10. Pivots to bunt correctly
——   ——   ——   11. Bends knees
——   ——   ——   12. Relaxes arms and grip
——   ——   ——   13. Gets on top of ball

Pitching

——   ——   ——   1. Control
——   ——   ——   2. Holds fingers on ball properly
——   ——   ——   3. Curve

Pitching

(1)	(2)	(3)	
_____	_____	_____	4. Fast ball
_____	_____	_____	5. Change-up
_____	_____	_____	6. (a) Rotation of ball on fast ball
_____	_____	_____	(b) Rotation of ball on curve ball
_____	_____	_____	7. Conceals pitches
_____	_____	_____	8. Stands on mound or rubber correctly
_____	_____	_____	9. Follows through, bends back
_____	_____	_____	10. Striding foot lands properly
_____	_____	_____	11. Pivot foot pivots correctly on rubber
_____	_____	_____	12. Keeps eye on target
_____	_____	_____	13. First base pick-off
_____	_____	_____	14. Second base pick-off
_____	_____	_____	15. Holds runners close to bag
_____	_____	_____	16. Throws to second on double play ball
_____	_____	_____	17. Checks position of teammates before delivery
_____	_____	_____	18. Backs up bases
_____	_____	_____	19. Covers first
_____	_____	_____	20. Fields position on batted ball
_____	_____	_____	21. Fielding bunts
_____	_____	_____	22. Keeps eye on wind

Catching

_____	_____	_____	1. Shifts well
_____	_____	_____	2. Gets rid of ball quickly
_____	_____	_____	3. No lost motion in steps of throw
_____	_____	_____	4. Throws well on double steal
_____	_____	_____	5. Can catch pop flies
_____	_____	_____	6. Picks up bunts with ease
_____	_____	_____	7. Uses one hand only when necessary
_____	_____	_____	8. Blocks home plate well
_____	_____	_____	9. Blocks pitches well
_____	_____	_____	10. Removes and throws mask properly
_____	_____	_____	11. Relaxes whole body when catching ball
_____	_____	_____	12. Hides signs—can switch signs
_____	_____	_____	13. Is good field general
_____	_____	_____	14. Weight on balls of feet

Catching

(1)	(2)	(3)	
——	——	——	15. Can tag properly
——	——	——	16. Calls pitches well
——	——	——	17. Uses voice
——	——	——	18. Checks defense before pitch
——	——	——	19. Backs up plays
——	——	——	20. Keeps eye on wind

Infield

——	——	——	1. Anticipates what to do with ball
——	——	——	2. Feet spread properly
——	——	——	3. Bends knees, keeps tail low
——	——	——	4. Weight on balls of feet
——	——	——	5. Uses cross-over step when breaking to sides
——	——	——	6. Fields ball out in front of body
——	——	——	7. Fields ball on side only when necessary
——	——	——	8. Relaxed wrists in fielding ball
——	——	——	9. Straightens up to throw only when necessary
——	——	——	10. Gets rid of ball quickly
——	——	——	11. Uses crow-hop or throws well without step
——	——	——	12. No hitch before throwing
——	——	——	13. Charges ball, does not let ball play him
——	——	——	14. Can make double play steps
——	——	——	15. Tags runner correctly
——	——	——	16. Can move to right and left well
——	——	——	17. Makes run-down play correctly
——	——	——	18. Uses voice to help teammates
——	——	——	19. Makes relays and cut-offs properly
——	——	——	20. Backs up plays
——	——	——	21. Keeps eye on the wind

Outfield

——	——	——	1. Gets jump on ball
——	——	——	2. Plays ground balls well
——	——	——	3. Gets in position to throw

Outfield

(1)	(2)	(3)	
____	____	____	4. Knows how to get set to throw
____	____	____	5. Throws low
____	____	____	6. Throws to proper bases
____	____	____	7. Anticipates running speed of base runners
____	____	____	8. Backs up bases and other fielders
____	____	____	9. Runs on toes
____	____	____	10. Uses voice to help teammates
____	____	____	11. Plays the fence well
____	____	____	12. Knows how to play sunny field
____	____	____	13. Hits cut-off and relay man consistently
____	____	____	14. Keeps eye on wind

Base Running

____	____	____	1. Runs on toes and is relaxed
____	____	____	2. Has high knee action
____	____	____	3. Body leans forward when running
____	____	____	4. Body leans in toward infield when making turn
____	____	____	5. When running straight line, feet are placed directly in front of nose
____	____	____	6. Elbows comfortably near body, bent nearly 90 degrees, uses pump action with arms
____	____	____	7. Uses cross-over step to break to bases
____	____	____	8. Rounds bases well
____	____	____	9. Takes enough lead
____	____	____	10. Is daring on base paths
____	____	____	11. Slides correctly
____	____	____	12. Slides all different ways
____	____	____	13. Knows how to break up double play
____	____	____	14. Uses good judgment
____	____	____	15. Runs with head up
____	____	____	16. Checks position of defense before each pitch
____	____	____	17. Watches wind
____	____	____	18. Looks at coach before rounding bases

Base Running

(1)   (2)   (3)

——   ——   ——   19. Knows number of outs
——   ——   ——   20. Watches preceding runners on base
hits and stolen bases

208. Running Performance—Time

Use Drill No. 196, Timed Base Running, preferably; however, Drill No. 19, Base Running for Time, can be used when timing base-running speed of players.

209. Throwing Performance

Purpose

To check the throwing abilities of players.

Procedure

A. *Outfielders and Infielders:*

1. Accuracy: After proper warm-up, at a distance of 150 feet, have players throw three times at a base. Use a fielder to back up the base.
2. Distance: When the players' arms are completely loose, have them throw twice for distance.

B. *Pitchers:*

Have pitchers throw to a catcher, who checks their fast ball, curve ball, and control. He also counts the number of strikes each pitcher throws.

210. Batting Performance

Purpose

To give the coach an opportunity to determine who can hit and who cannot.

Procedure

Let each batter bunt three balls down the third base line and three down the first base line. After he attempts the bunts, have him take four swings at balls thrown at medium speed and straight, then four swings at curve balls.

As an added skill test, have him hit several balls to the opposite field.

211. Fielding Performance in Position

Purpose

To give the coach an opportunity to learn to what degree candidates can play a position.

Procedure

Put players in the position they think they can play best and hit balls to them, giving them all possible plays that are likely to happen in that position. Use Multiple Infield Drill No. 121.

A. *Infield:*
1. Hit infielders all types of ground balls.
2. Hit all types of ground balls and have infielders make the different situation throws from that position.

B. *Outfield:*
1.–2. Same as infield. Field ground balls in outfield grass and make plays from their normal outfield position.
3. Hit outfielders all types of fly balls.
4. Hit them all types of fly balls and have them make the different situation throws from that position.

CHAPTER *17*

GIMMICKS

OF THE GAME

This could be one of the most important chapters of the book from a standpoint of helping the coach develop the individual player. All of these gimmicks have been used, and some are being used successfully by many coaches. They have been created or designed to *correct* a weakness or to *improve* a player's ability.

In view of the fact that most coaches are either the groundskeepers or the supervisors of the playing field, we have added a few ground tools designed by George Toma, the groundskeeper of the Kansas City Athletics. These tools are simple to make and are the basic tools needed to maintain a good field.

212. Batting Tee

The batting tee is useful for individual work. It should be placed with the ball in front of home plate, either outside, inside, or center, but *never on* home plate. Hitters must learn to meet the ball in front of the plate.

The batting tee is made by filling a five-gallon oil can three-fourths full of sand, placing one of three lengths of broomstick into the sand in an upright position, with a six- to eight-inch radiator hose over the top of the broomstick. The ball is placed on top of the radiator hose. There

ILLUS. NO. 27

should be three lengths of broomsticks: knee high, belt high, and letter high. Additional balls may be kept in the oil can for ready use.

When using the tee, balls can be hit against a canvas, mat, or hanging blanket, or they may be hit to a fielder. Some coaches use the tee to work infield and outfield drills. (Note Illustration No. 27, page 189.)

213. Whiffle Ball

The whiffle ball is slightly smaller than a baseball, made of plastic, hollow, with holes in one side only. Although ideal for indoor batting practice, *it should not be thrown by pitchers.* It can be used without damage to anything and can be hit with a full, powerful swing. Excellent for curve ball practice, the whiffle ball should be thrown at a distance of about 45 feet from the batter.

214. Cork Ball

Many major league baseball players have used or played with a cork ball. Made exactly like a baseball, the cork ball is slightly smaller than a tennis ball, but larger than a golf ball. It looks like a miniature baseball.

Ideal for outdoor batting practice, it makes the batter keep his eye on the ball. *It should not be thrown by pitchers.* The cork ball can be fielded just as a baseball is fielded and is very lively. Although it has tendency to sail when pitched, it can be thrown the regulation pitching distance.

215. Bottle Cap and Broomstick

Old bottle caps thrown and hit with a broomstick have developed the hitting eye of many major league players in their youth.

When thrown, a bottle cap does numerous tricks. In order to hit the cap, a player must keep his eye on it. It is thrown from a distance of about 30 to 45 feet from the batter. A half of a rubber ball also works well for this drill.

216. Sponge Rubber Practice Golf Balls

Many golfers use a soft sponge rubber ball for practice swings. They do not go far and can be used for batting practice to make the hitter keep his eye on the ball. Since they are light and are thrown from a distance of about 45 feet, *pitchers should not throw them.* Bat boys make the best pitchers for these balls. The balls cannot hurt anyone if hit by them, and bat boys enjoy striking out the varsity players.

217. Stuffed Stocking

(Note Drill No. 51.)

218. Ball Toss Fungo Batting

(Note Drill No. 47.)

219. Instructional Bunting Bat

This bat is made simply by cutting away that portion of the bat facing the pitched ball which, if hit with the ball, would make a poor bunt. The part removed is the top and bottom area around the trade mark and the top half of the head of the bat. In order to get the feeling of normal weight, after the bat has been cut and shaped, bore a ¾-inch hole six to eight inches deep in the head end of the bat, and fill it with lead. In order to keep the lead in and to prevent chipping, tape over and around the end of the bat. A nail or pin can be put through the bat and lead.

Practice with the bat causes the bunter to get on top of the ball. Bunters must be cautioned to keep the flat portion of the bat facing up at all times. (Note Illustration No. 28, page 192.)

220. Ball on Swinging Rope

Bore a ¼-inch hole through a ball, and pull a good strong rope through the hole with a fish-stringer. Tie a large knot in the end of the rope. At the other end of the rope, which is about 10 to 12 feet long, tie a portion of a bat handle. This is done by boring a ¼-inch hole ½-inch from the end of the portion of the bat away from the handle end, inserting the rope through the hole, and tying it.

ILLUS. NO. 28: Coach Danny Litwhiler with his instructional bunting bat. (See Gimmick No. 219.)

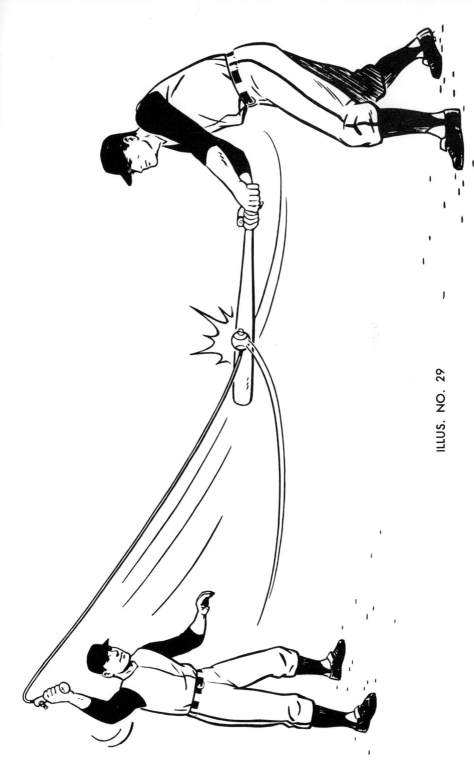

ILLUS. NO. 29

A player puts the bat handle in his hand and swings it around his head. At the perimeter of the circle made by the ball, a player attempts to hit the ball with a bat. A left handed swinger and a right handed swinger can get at opposite sides of the circle and attempt to hit the ball back and forth. This is good training for the eye and excellent practice for learning to hit the curve ball if the ball is swung in a steady circle. (Note Illustration No. 29, page 193.)

221. Hitting Tire

By hitting a tire with a bat, a player can develop the drive in his swing. The tire should be placed in front of the plate area so that it is in the position where the bat should meet the ball.

The tire can be suspended on a rope, braced against a wall, or built on a frame at strike zone height.

222. Lead Bat

Many coaches drill a hole lengthwise in the head end of a bat and fill it with lead. It usually is a ⅝- to a ¾-inch hole six to eight inches deep. Near the end of the bat, a nail or steel pin is driven through the wood and lead to hold the lead in place. To keep the bat from chipping, and as an added precaution to keep the lead in place, tape the bat end *thoroughly*. The lead could slip out when the bat is swung viciously.

This bat is normally used for pre-swing exercise before the player goes to bat. It tends to make the bat to be used feel lighter. A player can develop powerful and faster wrists for hitting by working with such a bat during the winter months, and the bat can be used during the season. It should be swung 50 to 100 times every day. The real function of the bat is to force the arms away from the body when the hitter is swinging.

223. Fifty-Ounce Bat

This is a regular bat made of the heaviest wood a bat company can use. It has a medium-sized handle, is 35 inches long, and weighs approximately 50 ounces.

The bat is used for swinging as in Drill No. 222 and is ideal for the Ball Toss Fungo Drill No. 47. Suitable for pepper games, it can also be used for slow-pitch batting practice. The bat teaches players how to swing while keeping their arms away from their body.

224. Multiple Batting Cage

As compared with the usual batting cage, which allows only one hitter and one pitcher to work, this batting cage is constructed so that many hitters and pitchers can work at the same time. (Note how it is used in Illustration No. 30, page 196.) Each batter is in his own stall and has his own pitcher outside the stall to throw to him. Only space and money dictate the number of stalls that can be built. It is recommended that a coach start with at least three stalls. Should he have a typical two-man cage, he can make a five-stall cage of it.

Providing a team maximum batting practice, the five-stall cage produces live batting practice in one day equal to five days of regular practice. Pitchers also get maximum work, plus the help they get in control development. Standing 48 feet away from the hole on the outside of the cage, pitchers must first throw the ball through the hole before it gets to the batter, who stands 12 feet behind the hole, in the stall. The hole in the net is three feet wide by four feet high, and the bottom of the hole is two feet off the ground. (Note Illustration No. 31, page 196.)

225. Balls Striped with Different Colors

Take four baseballs and paint a one-inch stripe of a standard but different color around each ball.

During batting practice, when a hitter comes to the plate, give the pitcher the colored balls. Without showing it to the hitter, the pitcher throws one of the balls. The batter swings at it but misses, then tells the catcher the color of the ball. If he calls three out of three colors correctly, he can hit four regular balls for practice. If he does not call them correctly, he loses his turn to hit.

This will make the hitter watch the ball while swinging the bat.

ILLUS NO. 30: The Florida State University batting cage.
(See *Gimmick No. 224.*)

ILLUS. NO. 31: Inside view of the Florida State University batting cage.
(See *Gimmick No. 224.*)

226. Testing Hitting Area of Bat

Not every bat has the same area of hitting surface. Players use sound to help them pick out the bat with the best wood and biggest hitting surface.

Take a bat in each hand, and hold one with the bottle-end up, perpendicular to the ground. Hold it loosely near the trade mark. Grasp the other bat in the same manner, but hold it parallel to the ground, at right angles to the other bat.

Starting at the hitting end and working toward the trade mark, begin hitting this bat against the other bat. Tap back and forth, and listen to the different sounds. The best hitting area produces the *solid* sound. Change bats and compare the sounds in order to choose the best bat.

227. "Assisto" Glove

The "Assisto" glove, now on the market, can be used to help teach a player to keep his hands on the bat as he completes his swing.

The glove is made with a wide strip of elastic attached to the back. With the hand and fingers placed around the bat in the desired position, the elastic is pulled down and around the fingers and snapped to the wrist just above the heel of the hand, permitting the thumb and index finger to remain free.

Since very few hitters remove the bottom hand during the swing, the glove is placed on the top hand, that is, the right hand for the right handed swinger and the left hand for the left handed swinger. (Note Illustration No. 32, page 198.)

228. Better Batting Grip

Beeswax rubbed on the handle of the bat and used with rosin gives a firm grip. Tar paper and pine tar are fair substitutes for beeswax. Powdered rosin does an adequate job, but rock rosin crushed and put in an old stocking is ideal.

Some players like to shave the bat handle with a broken bottle to get a slightly rougher grip.

SNAPS ON

198

229. String Target

Place two poles similar to volleyball standards four feet apart on either side of home plate, so that a string fastened to each pole will cross above the direct center of the plate. Tie three strings to the standards at different heights: one at armpit height, at waist height, and knee high respectively. At the center of the strings, directly over the center of the plate, tie a vertical string from the top horizontal string to the bottom one. Then, tie two other vertical strings so that one will come exactly to the edge of one side of home plate, and the other string will be at the opposite edge, making the distance between these outside strings the width of home plate.

This produces a window-type target at which the pichers can throw. It is a large rectangle the size of the strike zone divided into four smaller rectangles, one for each pitch: high inside, high outside, low inside, and low outside.

The strings should be taut, and the catcher should wear a mask when catching behind them.

230. Taped Mat Target

Hang a mat on the gym wall, and tape a strike zone target on it as suggested with the string target (Drill No. 229). If the wall is constructed of concrete or other material which is sturdy enough to withstand the blow of a thrown baseball, tape can be applied directly to the wall, or paint can be used.

231. Mirror for Pitching Practice

Many pitchers give something away in their movements, permitting numerous hitters to read them and tell what they are going to throw before they throw it. In order for the pitcher to see what the batter sees, we have developed a mirror * with which he can see his pre-pitch movements and delivery. The pitcher throws the ball at the mirror, which absorbs the blow and rebounds the ball to the pitcher.

* The author, on grounds that the construction of this mirror is too elaborate for the scope of this book, has promised to answer personally any queries concerning it. He may be contacted c/o Dept. of Phys. Education and Recreation, Florida State University.—Ed.

ILLUS. NO. 33

The mirror can also be useful to other players. It can be helpful to the outfielder in showing him what he is doing on his throws; it can help teach a catcher how to make the correct throw to second base, and batters can study their swings by watching their movements in the mirror. (Note Illustration No. 33, page 200.)

232. Eye Patch Drill

If a pitcher is having poor control, he probably is taking his focus eye off the catcher or target. Every person has a focus or dominant eye. It can be found by pointing at an object as if the finger were a gun, aiming with both eyes open. Close first one eye, then the other. One eye will be aiming at the target, and the other will be off the target. The eye on the target is the focus eye. By putting an eye patch over the non-focus eye, the focus eye does the job for pitcher. Have him throw easily like this for a short time, and then have him throw hard for several times. Do this daily until he learns to hold his focus eye on the target and his control gets better.

233. Yo-Yo Pitching Drill

It is possible to develop a curve ball by using a good yo-yo. If a pitcher has a very poor curve ball and the coach cannot teach him the mechanics of a curve, he can improve through using a yo-yo. Put the pitcher on the rubber, and have him assume the wind-up stance with the yo-yo in his hand. He takes his wind-up and follows through slowly with his delivery. As he comes through with his arm and hand, they follow the same path taken when throwing a ball. When the hand gets about at his head, he bends and shortens his arm. His palm is facing his face, and the yo-yo is held by the thumb, middle, and index fingers, so that it will roll off the side of the index finger, down toward his feet. This is an exaggerated way of spinning a ball for a curve. The yo-yo should go straight downward and spin at the end of the string. The pitcher should jerk it up and start all over again. After this action has been mastered, he should assume a set stance and go through the motion with his arm and hand. Soon, he should have a much better curve ball.

234. Iron or Lead Ball

Some players have made a mold of a regulation baseball and used it for molding a heavy metal ball. The ball is used during the off-season for the Pillow Throw Drill No. 235, and also for general wrist development. However, the ball is not used for making actual throws, since this could injure the arm. For throwing, a ball can be made slightly heavier than a regulation ball.

235. Pillow Throw Drill

During the winter months or off-season, players can aid in the development of the wrist snap by throwing or snapping a ball into a pillow at close range. Three to four feet from the pillow is a good range for the throw.

236. Rope for Snap Throw

Take a rope that is three feet long and one-half inch in diameter, and tie a knot in one end. With the knot end free, hold the rope back in the position the hand takes when going back to throw a ball. *Example:* The catcher holds the rope in his hand beside his right ear, and the rope hangs behind his back. He brings his hand and arm forward, making the rope snap out in front of him. His wrist action should be like that used in throwing a baseball. If the rope snaps, the wrist action is good. (Note Illustration No. 34, page 203.)

237. Baton Weight Wind-Up

Bore a quarter-inch hole through the center of a round piece of wood which is 12 inches long and 1½ inches in diameter. Pass a strong cord through the hole and tie it. At the other end of the cord, which is three feet long, tie a weight of 10 to 20 pounds.

Hold the wooden handle, or baton, by both hands; lift it up and away from the chest, begin to move the hands and wrists so that the cord winds around the wood. Then, reverse the motion of the weight so that the cord unwinds. This drill will develop the wrists and forearms. (Note Illustration No. 35, page 204.)

ILLUS. NO. 34

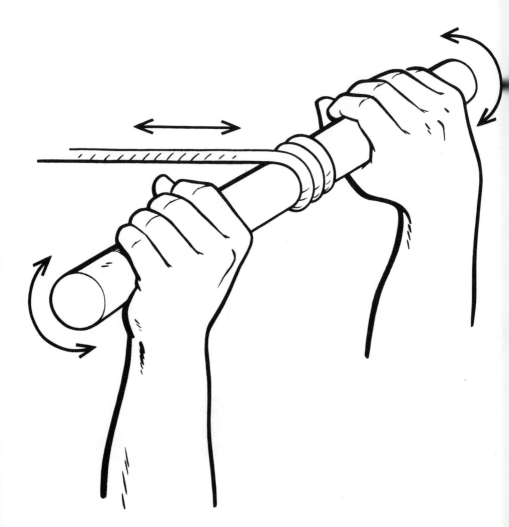

ILLUS. NO. 35

17"

6"

ILLUS. NO. 36

238. Rope Pull Arm Strengthener

(Note Drill No. 28 and Illustration No. 6, page 24.)

239. Rolla-Rolla Board (Note Illustration No. 36, page 205.)

This gimmick is excellent to develop the muscles for the side movements of players. It is particularly good for catchers, third basemen, and first basemen, but is very good for all players. After the player has learned the art of using the board with the aid of another person, or leaning his hands against a wall, and he has learned to balance himself on the board, have him put a glove on and toss balls to his right and left. He should attempt to field the ball and keep his balance.

We call it a Rolla-Rolla board; however, it may be known as a "Bongo" board on the market. It is composed of three parts which can be made if one is not available.

1. The top board is 30 inches long and made of ¾-inch plywood, 12 inches wide. On the bottom side, on each end, attach one-inch triangular strips of wood. On the top side where the feet are placed, glue six-inch strips of rubber mat for better footing. Also cover bottom side with rubber mat to prevent cylinder from slipping.
2. The bottom board is 36 inches long and 12 inches wide, and made of ¾-inch plywood. The end strips are the same as those on the top board, but attached to the top side of the board. Use same type rubber material as above to cover the top side to prevent the cylinder from slipping.
3. The cylinder that works between the two boards is seventeen inches long and six inches in diameter. It is made by gluing or laminating four pieces of 2" by 8" board long enough to place in a lathe for turning and cutting with a wood chisel.

240. Stuffed Glove

Take an old catching glove and stuff it so that it has no pocket. The material used should be something that will not form a pocket, such as a product called "Absorblo."

Have fielders practice fielding with the glove. Whereas the good fielder gives with the ball when fielding it, the poor fielder kicks many balls out of the glove. Since many balls are missed while using this glove, fielders will get practice in scrambling for the ball to throw the runner out. Fielders will learn to use two hands on the ball.

It is an excellent glove for teaching the catcher to use two hands, and is excellent for use in double play practice.

241. "Diamond Dust"

"Diamond Dust" is a product used for drying a ball that gets wet in the grass or a puddle of water. If used immediately, the ball is ready for play within 25 seconds. By working the dust around a wet ball with a brush and wiping it with a towel, you can have the ball dry almost immediately.

242. "Diamond Grit"

This is a sand-like product used to condition a wet infield. With very little effort by the groundskeeper, "Diamond Grit," when raked into wet dirt, puts any field or spot on the field in excellent playing shape. The area can be soupy, but with the application of this grit it is ready for play within a few minutes.

243. Spray Drag

Most coaches have very little time or man-power with which to get a field ready for the game after practice. A machine can be made which will spray and drag an infield in less than five minutes, and it needs only two men pushing and a third man helping.

Between a set of two pairs of wheels we suspended a 40-foot triangular TV antenna and stretched three sprinkler-type hoses through the antenna. Proper couplings produced an ideal sprinkling system 40 feet long. Approximately five feet in front of the front wheels we placed a brace on each set of wheels to hold a double length of one-inch hose stretched between the pairs of wheels for dragging. For pushing purposes, we put lawn mower-type handles on each set of wheels. The front wheels of each set of wheels are swiveled, and the back wheels are stationary.

The drag can be pushed or pulled back and forth to give the field a good conditioning. The three sprinkler-type hoses water the field and the double length hose drags the field.

244. Spike Drag

Every field needs a daily raking and working of the topsoil in the skinned area. An ideal tool can be made by building a drag 36 inches square. The following materials are needed: three two-by-fours each three feet long, three one-by-fours each three feet long, two one-by-twos each three feet long; approximately 130 spikes five inches long, and some rope with which to pull the drag.

Directions:

1. Bore holes slightly smaller than the spikes, two rows in each two-by-four, one inch from the edges and one inch apart. No hole is directly behind or beside another.
2. Drive the spikes through the holes, and nail the one-by-fours on top of the heads of the spikes.
3. On the ends of the two-by-fours, nail the one-by-twos. The first two-by-four is at one end; the second one is in the middle, and the third one is at the other end. This results in a three-foot-by-three-foot spike drag.
4. At the ends of a two-by-four (that is, at the corners of the drag), attach a rope for pulling. Then, the spike side will cut the dirt, and by reversing the drag, the flat side of the one-by-fours can be used for floating or leveling the dirt.

245. Board Float

Every infield needs a good float to level the skinned area of the field. This can be made by shiplapping three 2" by 12" planks eight feet long. Tie a rope for pulling on the ends of the plank that is used for the bottom to start the shiplapping. The planks overlap approximately four inches on each other.

246. Cotton Textile Apron Drag

Coaches located near a cotton textile mill or machine company may find an old apron, which may be three or more feet wide and up to twelve feet long. This apron is made of wooden slats, either plain or with many spikes or needles in the slats.

The apron with spikes in the slats does an excellent job of dragging the skinned field, and the plain one works equally well in leveling the field.

247. First Base Protection Screen

When he is covering the base for infielders fielding ground balls between pitches, during batting practice, the first baseman needs protection from batted balls.

A screen for this purpose should be approximately seven feet high and five feet wide. It can be made of a framework of ¾" pipe or two-by-fours, and is held up by two free-swinging legs. It is covered with heavy chicken wire.

248. Pitcher Protection Screen

Some coaches like to protect the batting practice pitcher from the batted ball. However, the screen is used mostly for non-pitchers such as the coach and fielders. The screen is made of a framework of either ¾" pipe or two-by-fours, covered by fine chicken wire. It is four feet high and five feet wide, and is held upright by two free-swinging legs.

249. Rubber Bases for Indoors

Cut bases of actual regulation dimensions out of rubber floor runners. They can be painted white and will not slip when used indoors. On road trips a rubber home plate can be carried along for use in the bull pen where one is not provided.

250. Indoor Pitching Mound

With a few pieces of scrap wood and two plywood shets of ¾", 4' by 8', an indoor pitching mound frame can be constructed. To complete the mound, one will also need some thin strips of foam rubber and a sufficient amount of "Laykold," "Grasstex," or similar asphalt-like material used in the construction of all-weather tracks and tennis courts to cover the frame two inches thick.

Directions:

1. Cut lengthwise two ¾" plywood four-by-eights.
   a. Cut one piece in half, making two pieces two feet wide.
   b. Cut the other large piece of plywood into two pieces, one three feet wide and the other one foot wide.
2. Butt the three-foot piece and one of the two-foot pieces lengthwise side by side. You now have a five-foot-by-eight-foot board, which serves as the sloping area from the rubber toward home. (Note Illustration No. 37, Isometric View, page 211.)
3. The other two-foot piece is cut five feet long, making the flat area at the rubber where the pitcher stands while in his wind-up stance. (Note Illustration No. 37, Plan View.)
4. To get height for the mound, use two 2" by 12" by five-foot pieces of board under the two-foot-by-five-foot pieces in instruction 3. (Note Illustration No. 37, Side View.)
5. Across the front edge, toward the catcher, nail on the bottom a 2" by 6" by five-foot plank. This makes the slope from the rubber to the front of the mound.
6. Three partitions or braces must go crosswise under the long eight-by-five-foot board at two-foot intervals. These braces are *one*, 2" by 7½" by five feet; *one*, 2" by 9" by five feet, and *one*, 2" by 10½" by five feet. (Note Illustration No. 37, Side View.) It must be braced on the sides from front to back, preferably with ¾" plywood. The one-foot strip which was cut off in instruction 1-B and the piece left from instruction 3 can be used, plus a scrap piece to complete the job. For the finished construction, see Illustration No. 37, Isometric View.
7. At the center of the two-foot-by-five-foot board (instruction 3) is placed a 2" by 6" by two-foot board for the pitching rubber. It is placed on the edges where the two boards meet and the slope begins. (Note Illustration No. 37, either Isometric or Plan View.)

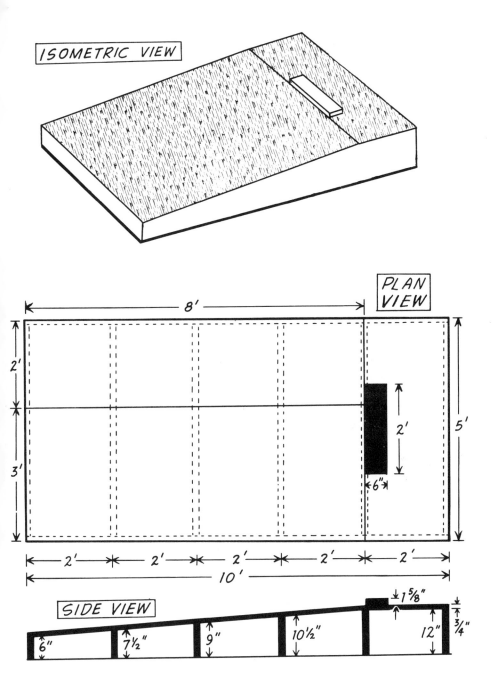

ISOMETRIC VIEW

PLAN VIEW

8'

2'

3'

2'

5'

6"

2' 2' 2' 2' 2'

10'

SIDE VIEW

1 5/8"

6" 7½" 9" 10½" 12" 3/4"

ILLUS. NO. 37

211

8. Cover the board mound the thickness of the pitching rubber (two inches) with an asphalt-like material, and taper this covering to zero inches at the edges of the mound. The best covering materials are those mentioned earlier, or other similar products.
9. For protection of the gym floor and to prevent slipping, glue a covering of foam rubber to the bottom edges of the frame, and lay a tarpaulin under it so that the tarp extends well out from under the frame. This will catch any material which might come off the mound.
10. Pitchers will use shoes with golf spikes, or they will use gym shoes. Track spikes $\frac{1}{8}''$ long would be ideal.

251. Helmets

On the market there is a helmet designed primarily for the protection of the hitter. Many coaches find that it is good protection for players in the field or while running the bases. They require the helmet to be worn at all times. It gives the hitters more confidence, and, if worn at all times, it is not a distraction at the plate. Helmets will last many years when used in this manner. Therefore, they are economical. However, when they are thrown around from hitter to hitter, they soon wear out.

CHAPTER 18

ORGANIZATION FOR ONE DIAMOND OR PRACTICE AREA

It is of prime importance for a baseball coach to keep his players busy every minute of a practice session in order to impress upon them that they have to work before they can become a winning team.

It is necessary to have a set pattern for practice so the players will know what they are supposed to be doing every minute. The coach's mind must be flexible to take weather and last-minute developments into consideration.

The coach must think in terms of the player and how to get the most out of him. When a player comes on the field, the first thing he wants to do is either throw or bat a ball, and he should be permitted to start his practice this way. Since these are the most important fundamentals of the game, they should be done first in practice.

252. Loosening-Up Period: 15 Minutes

As soon as they come onto the field, the outfielders and infielders should begin organized pepper games. Pitchers and catchers should begin working together. They should all be doing some type of loosening-up, running, throwing or calisthenics.

Suggested Drills: Nos. 12, 14-16, 20-24, 27, 29, 117.

253. Batting Practice: 60 Minutes

Here is where a coach can get the most out of a practice. While the batters are taking their licks (no more than two on deck at a time), the extra pitchers and catchers should be assigned to infield and outfield fungoing. At first this practice may appear chaotic, but if it is properly arranged the player who is hitting the fungos to the infield will learn to time his hits so they are made between pitches to the plate.

Meanwhile, the infielders are learning to field the ball off the bat at the plate, in addition to the fungos. It sharpens their wits and keeps them busy all the time.

Infielders, outfielders and catchers should alternate daily as to who hits first. Pitchers may be included in this practice by giving them the first ten minutes.

Suggested Drills to aid batting practice: Nos. 97-99.

254. Fielding in Position: 10 Minutes

After batting practice the coaches, managers and pitchers who hit good fungos should be assigned a position in the infield where they can hit the ball in rapid succession for about 10 minutes. During this time every fielder will receive individual attention from the coach, who can point out his fielding weaknesses and work with him to correct them.

While this part of the practice is going on, fungo hitters are assigned to hitting to the outfielders. The catchers are working along the sidelines on pop flies, blocking the ball, shifting to either side to handle wild pitches and working on bunts.

Suggested Drills: Nos. 36, 117, 121-123.

255. Fundamentals of Play: 20 Minutes

After fielding practice, everyone should be called and instructed to work on the general fundamentals of the game such as sliding, base running, actual bunt situations, pick-offs, cut-off plays, run-down plays, the defense and offense of the delayed and double steals, and handling of pop-ups by the infield and outfield.

Considerable time should be spent on pop-ups. All the players should learn to distinguish each other's voices and know who should be the one to make the catch. The value of Drill 37 cannot be underestimated. Many games are lost because of a mix-up on a seemingly easy pop fly.

256. Outfield-Infield Practice: 10 Minutes

The regular infield practice, with the outfielders making their throws to the bases and the infielders throwing around the horn, should be started.

The outfielders should throw in from the outfield first. The left fielder throws three or more throws to second base and the same to home. He can fake some throws to third and throw to second. The center fielder makes his throws to third and home, faking to third and throwing to second. The right fielder throws to third and home, faking to second and throwing to first. The first baseman cuts off the throws to home from the right fielder and the center fielder. The third baseman cuts off the throws to home from the left fielder. The shortstop cuts off the throws to third base from the center fielder and right fielder.

The outfielders can either run after the throws or continue fielding fly balls. The infielders now take over with all the enthusiasm they can put forth. The coach should have a routine way of hitting infield and a routine way of throwing the ball around. Use this same system prior to all games. It keeps a team from looking lost on the field.

Suggested Drills to aid practice: Nos. 39-41, 122-123.

257. Running: 5 Minutes

The five-minute running is used for the infielders. The outfielders will have run about 10 minutes. The catchers run according to what work they have in infield practice. The pitchers have a 15-minute running session. This running session must be made as enjoyable as possible. No player likes to run just for the sake of running; he usually thinks of running as a pill he has to take with every practice.

Suggested Drills: Nos. 11, 13, 193-198, 200-203.

258. Alternate Practice Sessions

Once the team is in shape to play, the above practice session should be used on alternate days (Monday, Wednesday, and Friday). Games or scrimmages should be held on Tuesday, Thursday, and Saturday. In case of rain the coach should decide which is needed most, games or practice.

Suggested Drills for game practice: Nos. 43-45.

CHAPTER 19

PRE-SEASON

DAILY PRACTICE

SCHEDULE—

INDOORS

There are certain drills and fundamentals which cannot be executed indoors. Therefore, the goal for indoor practice is to avoid these and work with drills and fundamentals which are adaptable for indoor performance, and are necessary for the development of the team. Thus, time will be saved for the drills and fundamentals which can only be done outdoors. It is advisable to have a watch or alarm clock to time the activities. This will help the coach keep on schedule.

One week prior to the first day of practice, the coach should call a meeting of all candidates for the team. At this time he explains the practice plans, training rules, prospects of the team, equipment necessary, and what he expects of the team in general.

In the daily practice charts, the following symbols have been used to designate player positions:

O-*outfield*; I-*infield*; C-*catcher*; P-*pitcher*; 1B-*first base*; 2B-*second base*; 3B-*third base*; SS-*shortstop*. The numerals indicate the numbers of the drills to be used.

For example: P-C:85 means that catchers catch pitchers, who work on their rhythm. (Drill No. 85 is a rhythm drill for pitchers.)

TIME	FIRST DAY MONDAY	SECOND DAY TUESDAY	THIRD DAY WEDNESDAY	FOURTH DAY THURSDAY	FIFTH DAY FRIDAY
4:00	ALL PLAYERS: Run around the gym	SAME	SAME	SAME	SAME
4:05	ALL PLAYERS: Drill 88	SAME	SAME	SAME	SAME
4:15	ALL PLAYERS: Drill 117	SAME	SAME	SAME	SAME
4:25	P: 229-230 OTHERS: 29	SAME	SAME	SAME	SAME
4:40	P-C: 85, 91 O: 34, 179 I: Hitting 212-213, 216, 217-A, 221	SAME	P-C: 93, 109 OTHERS: Same as Monday	P-C: 91, 104, 109 OTHERS: Same as Monday	P-C: 32, 85, 104, 109 OTHERS: Same as Monday
4:55	P: 12 C: 102, 105 O: 212-213, 216, 217-A, 221 I: 34, 116	P: 14 C: 106 O: Same as Monday I: 34, 116	P: 12 C: 113 O: Same as Monday I: 34, 116	P: 14 C: 102-105-A,B O: Same as Monday I: 34, 116	P: 12 C: 106 O: Same as Monday I: 34, 116
5:10	P-C: 77, 85, 91 O: 178 I: 31-32	P-C: 84 O: 181 I: 31-32	P-C: 86, 104 O: 186 I: 31, 32	P-C: 84 O: 182-183 I: 31-32	P-C: 77, 85, 91 O: 178 I: 31-32
5:20	P: 29 C: 212-213, 216 217-A, 221 O: 182 I: 34, 118	P: 83 C: Same as Monday O: 178 I: 34, 118	P: 81 C: Same as Monday O: 181 I: 119	P: 80 C: Same as Monday O: 178 I: 126	P: 82 C: Same as Monday O: 181 I: 118
5:30	P: 95 C: 107 O: 183 I: 120	P: 29 C: 112 O: 182-183 I: 119	P: 29 C: 102 O: 177 (Thrown Ball) I: 118	P: 29 C: 107 O: 181 I: 120	P: 29 C: 107 O: 182-183 I: 126
5:45	P: 11, 4 C-I: 205, 11 O: 27, 11	SAME	SAME	SAME	SAME

TIME	SIXTH DAY MONDAY	SEVENTH DAY TUESDAY	EIGHTH DAY WEDNESDAY	NINTH DAY THURSDAY	TENTH DAY FRIDAY
4:00	ALL PLAYERS: Run around gym	SAME	SAME	SAME	SAME
4:05	ALL PLAYERS: Loosen up-throw	SAME	SAME	SAME	SAME
4:15	ALL PLAYERS: 117	SAME	SAME	SAME	SAME
4:25	P: 229-230 ALL OTHERS: Pepper Games	SAME	SAME	P: 197-198 ALL OTHERS: Pepper Games	P: 229-230 ALL OTHERS: Pepper Games
4:40	P-2B-SS: 95 3B-1B: 133, 168, 169 C-O: 212, 213, 216, 217-A, 221	P-C: 85, 91, 93 104, 109 O: 177 I: 118	P-C: 93, 104, 109 O: 64-68 I: 31-32	P: 82 O: 183 I: 133, 141, 156, 168	P-C: 77, 93, 104, 109 O: 212-213, 216, 217-A, 221 I: 118
4:55	P-C: 74, 77, 92 O: 179 I: 212, 213, 216, 217-A, 221	P: 14 O: 34, 179 I: 212-213, 216, 217-A, 221 C: 113	P: 12 O: 182-183 I: 116 C: 64-68	P: 14 O: 34, 179 I: 212, 213, 216, 217-A, 221 C: 113	P: 12 C: 199 I-O: Explain and go through 129-E,F, 138-D, 154-E, 170-D,186
5:10	P: 12 C: 102 O: 178 I: 116	P-C: 103 O: 182 I: 120	P-C: 82, 113 O: 34, 179 I: 64-68	P-C: 84 O: 212-213, 216, 217-A, 221 I: 121	P-C: 108 I-O: Continue above drills
5:20	P: 29 C: 106, 105-A,B O: 183 I: 120	P: 29 C-O: 212, 213, 216, 217-A,221 2B-SS-1B: 157-158 3B: 119-B	P: 64-68 C-1B-3B: 134, 173-B, 106-F O: 197-198 2B-SS: 145, 157	P: 64-68 C: 107 O: 199 I: 212-213, 216, 217-A, 221	P: 64-68 C-1B-3B: 106-F, 134, 173-B 2B-SS: 145, 157 O: 197-198
5:30	P: 80 C: 107 O: 180 (Throw Ball) I: 119-A,B	P-3B: 82-C, 168-D C: 102, 106 O: 180 2B-SS-1B: 145-146	P: 95-A C: 95-A with Pitchers O: 180 (Throw Ball) I: 197-198	P: 199 C: 110 I-O: 120	P: 29 C-I: 212, 213, 216, 217-A, 221 O-182-183
5:45	P: 11, 4 C-I: 205, 11 O: 27 then 11	SAME	SAME	SAME	SAME

219

CHAPTER 20

PRE-SEASON DAILY PRACTICE SCHEDULE— OUTDOORS

If possible, a team should have at least two or three weeks of outdoor drills before the first game. If the team has been practicing indoors, the coach must be certain to cover the drills and fundamentals that could not be covered, such as actual ground balls in the dirt, sliding in the dirt or grass, fly balls and pop flies, long hard throws, cut-off and relay plays, the double play, base running, batting practice, and practice games.

The coach who is going outdoors for his first practice session can go along very well with the drills listed here. However, his players should have been running and throwing on their own time for at least two weeks prior to the first day of practice. The first day should be a good, big practice session.

The second week of practice initiates practice game situations. A pitching rotation for the pitchers who will be pitching the regular season games should be started in the third week. The starting lineup should be working and playing games together. Particular attention should be paid to starting pitchers, double play work, pop flies, base running, and the batting order.

During batting practice and practice games, the coach should be looking for the following factors in his hitters—things that should help him determine his batting order which should be made up according to hitters' abilities with the bat and their base running:

1. The lead-off man should be a good base-on-balls man, hit singles, get on base often, and have good speed.
2. The second hitter should be a good bunter, fair hitter, and be fast enough to beat the double play. Preferably, he should be a left handed hitter.
3. The third hitter must have fair speed and fair power with the bat. He must be a good hitter of doubles and triples. Being left handed also has its advantages.
4. The fourth hitter is the clean-up hitter. He should have power and be a good hitter. His hits should be long fly balls and home runs. He need not be a fast runner.
5. The fifth hitter is the second clean-up hitter with power, and he must be a good hitter. However, speed is not too important.
6. The sixth hitter is sometimes called the second lead-off hitter. He must be able to bunt and be a good hit-and-run man. Speed is important.
7. The seventh hitter must also be a good bunter and hit-and-run man. Speed is important.
8. Usually, the eighth hitter is the catcher, but not necessarily a weak hitter. He should have the power necessary to score a man from first base.
9. The ninth hitter usually is the pitcher, but is also the weakest hitter. He must be an excellent bunter.

In the daily practice charts, the following symbols have been used to designate player positions:

O-*outfield*; I-*infield*; C-*catcher*; P-*pitcher*; 1B-*first base*; 2B-*second base*; 3B-*third base*; SS-*shortstop*. The numerals indicate the numbers of the drills to be used. For example: P:11 means that pitchers do Drill No. 11, football pass drill for running.

TIME	FIRST DAY MONDAY	SECOND DAY TUESDAY	THIRD DAY WEDNESDAY	FOURTH DAY THURSDAY	FIFTH DAY FRIDAY
4:00	ALL PLAYERS: General Loosening up - Throwing	SAME	SAME	SAME	SAME
4:05	ALL PLAYERS: Pepper Games	P-C: Starting Batting Practice Warm up ALL OTHERS: Pepper Games	SAME	SAME	SAME
4:15	P-C: Play Catch Pepper Games SCREEN CANDIDATES 208, 209, 211	BATTING PRACTICE: 62, 97-99 I: Ground Balls O: Fly Balls C: Catch Batting Practice, Warm up Pitcher P: 12, 14, 15	SAME	SAME	SAME
5:15	P-C: Batting Practice SCREEN CANDIDATES 210	P: 80 OTHERS: 27, 117	P: 82 OTHERS: 27, 117	P: 81 OTHERS: 27, 117	I: 200 P: 79 C-O: 27, 117
5:30	CONTINUE DRILL 210	P: Hit to I-O O: 34, 179, 180 I: 121 C: 114	SAME	SAME	C-O: 200 P-I: 121
5:45	CONTINUE DRILL 210	P: 11 or 13 I-C-O: 205 and 11	SAME	SAME	P: 200 I-C-O: 205, 11
6:00	RUN AROUND FIELD SHOWER	SHOWER	SHOWER	SHOWER	SHOWER

TIME	SIXTH DAY MONDAY	SEVENTH DAY TUESDAY	EIGHTH DAY WEDNESDAY	NINTH DAY THURSDAY	TENTH DAY FRIDAY
4:00	ALL PLAYERS: General Loosening up - Throwing	SAME	SAME	SAME	SAME
4:05	P-C: Starting Batting Practice Begin Warm up OTHERS: Pepper Games	SAME	P-C: Starting One Pitch Game, Warm up-43 Begin Warm up OTHERS: Pepper Games	P-C: Warm up for Batting Practice OTHERS: Pepper Games	P-C: Starting one Pitch Game, Warm up-43 OTHERS: Pepper Games
4:15	Batting Practice 62, 97-99 I: 34,116,145-146, 157-158 O: 34,179,182-183 P-C: Catch Batting Practice 74,77,85,92	SAME as Monday O: Add 181, 185	Play One Pitch Game: 43 Make Substitutions OTHERS: 29,64,71, 200 P: 74,77,85,92-93, 12,14,15 C: 102-109, 114	Batting Practice 62, 97-99 I: 34,116,145-146, 157,158 P-C: 74,77,85,92 O: 34,179,181,185	Play One Pitch Game: 43 Make Substitu- tions OTHERS: 29,64-71, 200 P: 74,77,85,92-93, 12,14,15 C: 102-109, 114
5:15	P: 79 OTHERS: 27 and 117	P-C: 84 OTHERS: 27, 117	CONTINUE GAME	P-C: 82, 113 OTHERS: 27 and 117	CONTINUE GAME
5:30	P: Hit to I-O O: 189 I: 121, 132, 163 C: 114	ALL PLAYERS: 112 and 95	CONTINUE GAME	ALL PLAYERS: 112 and 95	CONTINUE GAME
5:45	P: 11 or 13 OTHERS: 186, 135, 151, 164, 172-D	P: 11 or 13 I-C-O: 124 and 11	ALL PLAYERS NOT PLAYING: 11 or 13	P: 11 or 13 I-C-O: 205 and 11	ALL PLAYERS NOT PLAYING: 11 or 13
6:00	SHOWER	SHOWER	SHOWER	SHOWER	SHOWER

223

TIME	ELEVENTH DAY MONDAY	TWELFTH DAY TUESDAY	THIRTEENTH DAY WEDNESDAY	FOURTEENTH DAY THURSDAY	FIFTEENTH DAY FRIDAY
4:00	ALL PLAYERS: General Loosening up - Throwing	SAME	SAME	SAME	SAME
4:05	P-C: Starting Two Pitch Game, Begin Warming up-44 OTHERS: Pepper Games	P-C: Starting Batting Practice, Begin Warm up OTHERS: Pepper Games	GAME: 44 SAME AS MONDAY	PRACTICE SAME AS TUESDAY	GAME: 45 SAME AS MONDAY
4:15	Play Two Pitch Game: 44 OTHERS: 29,64-71, 200 P: 74,77,85,92-93, 12,14,15 C: 102-109, 114	Batting Practice 62, 97-99 OTHERS: Repeat Ninth Day Drills	GAME SAME AS MONDAY USE SUBSTITUTES FOR GAME	SAME AS TUESDAY	GAME: Six Outs - 45 OTHERS: SAME AS MONDAY USE SUBSTITUTES
5:15	CONTINUE GAME	P-I: 95,131,150, 161,173 C: 134 O: Run for Pick-Offs	CONTINUE GAME	P: 80-81 C: 114 I: 121 O: 178-180	CONTINUE GAME
5:30	CONTINUE GAME	CONTINUE ABOVE DRILLS	CONTINUE GAME	P-1B: 83 C: 113 3B: 168 SS-2B: 145, 157	CONTINUE GAME
5:45	ALL PLAYERS NOT PLAYING: 11 or 13	P: 11 or 13 I-C-O: 205 and 11	SAME AS MONDAY	SAME AS TUESDAY	SAME AS MONDAY
6:00	SHOWER	SHOWER	SHOWER	SHOWER	SHOWER

224

THE
COACHING
CHALLENGE

There are numerous challenges left for all coaches. A real need exists for new ideas in baseball. There is a tendency to do things because someone else did them. There may even be fear to try new things because of possible criticism. Here are a few suggested pertinent problems.

Much can be learned about preparing a baseball field for practice and games. The coach must be a good groundskeeper if he wants his players to be good fielders. One must know about muscle strength, reaction and coordination. Too little is known about the eyes, for instance.

Research can be made in the field of tachistoscope training to aid umpires and players alike. They should be able to react faster and diagnose a play faster with this training. Would a speed reading course with this flash meter machine help players?

How much is known about the eye and its job in hitting? One cannot hit if he cannot see, but what other factors should be considered?

Does the color of the eye have anything to do with hitting? It is known that light-eyed persons are more subject to eye strain, and that their eyes do not adjust readily to light changes. Blonds are more sensitive to sun glare, and cannot see nearly so well at night.

Do fellows like Ted Williams and Stan Musial hit better than the average player because they have better depth perception, peripheral vision and binocular vision? Why do they have better ability to see a moving object and interpret what they see faster and easier than the average hitter? It is a known fact that a moving eye sees nothing, that it must be motionless in order to see. Do the good hitters hold their eyes motionless when hitting?

Working on these problems will keep one from worrying solely about winning or losing—but solve any one of them and it may be possible to win more games than you think!

INDEX

The following index is arranged *alphabetically* according to the chapter titles in the book and according to subject matter in each chapter.

The *numbers listed* are the *drill numbers*.

BASE RUNNING (*cont.*)

CHAPTER 4

BATTING

CHAPTER 5

BUNTING

CHAPTER 7

CATCHING

CHAPTER 2

CONDITIONING

CHAPTER 8

INFIELD

CHAPTER 18

ORGANIZATION FOR ONE DIAMOND OR PRACTICE AREA

CHAPTER 13

OUTFIELD

OUTFIELD (*cont.*)

CHAPTER 6

PITCHING

PITCHING *(cont.)*

CHAPTER 15

PRE-GAME PRACTICE

CHAPTER 19

PRE-SEASON PRACTICE—INDOORS

CHAPTER 20

PRE-SEASON PRACTICE—OUTDOORS

CHAPTER 16

SCREENING CANDIDATES

CHAPTER 10

SECOND BASE

CHAPTER 11

SHORTSTOP

CHAPTER 3

TEAM DRILLS

CHAPTER 12

THIRD BASEMAN